Barb Parker fleshes out for us what it's like to come alongside one's ailing and aging parents and support them in the closing chapter of their lives. Her openness and transparency as she writes what it's like to be there for them every step of the way will leave the reader in awe as well as a little teary-eyed. This is a must-read for all who find themselves at this point in their lives, whether as a caregiver or one being cared for by a close family member.

—Sandra Norton
friend and author of *Finding Me*

As someone who was a caregiver to my late husband, I can relate to this story as it unfolds. The way this book is written provides the perspective of a position not everyone has to experience.

I recommend this book to all readers. It will draw you in, show you the experiences, and challenge you. It's not easy: the challenge is real as each day brings new obstacles to overcome.

You need to be a strong person to be someone's primary caregiver, and an even stronger person to be a caregiver to one who gave you life, raising and caring for you.

My Mum is a strong woman. Maybe that's where I got it. She cared for Gram for seven years and stayed with her until Gram drew her last breath.

Rest in peace, Gram.
—Karla Kennedy

Don't Leave Me

Barb Parker

DON'T LEAVE ME
Copyright © 2024 by Barb Parker

All rights reserved. Neither this publication nor any part of this publication may be reproduced or transmitted in any form or by any means, electronic or mechanical, including photocopying, recording or any information storage and retrieval system, without permission in writing from the author.

ISBN: 978-1-4866-2610-6
eBook ISBN: 978-1-4866-2611-3

Word Alive Press
119 De Baets Street Winnipeg, MB R2J 3R9
www.wordalivepress.ca

Cataloguing in Publication information can be obtained from Library and Archives Canada.

Contents

Dedication	vii
Introduction	ix
One: I Can't Breathe	1
Two: One Day at a Time	5
Three: Last Call	9
Four: What About Mum	15
Five: Yellow Socks and Purple Onions	19
Six: The Fall	23
Seven: Time for a Change	27
Eight: Fitting In	31
Nine: The Flu	41
Ten: Too Old for Surgery?	45
Eleven: The Broken Chair	49
Twelve: Call 911	57

Thirteen: The New Bed	61
Fourteen: Don't Sass Me	65
Fifteen: Broken	67
Sixteen: It Took Her Breath Away	71
Seventeen: Day Six	75
Eighteen: Her Wish	79
Nineteen: Is She Sleeping?	81
Twenty: Take the Picture	83
Twenty-One: Family and Friends	85
Twenty-Two: Feathers from Heaven	87
Conclusion	91
Appendix: Memories of a Special Lady	95
Mum's Molasses Cookies	123

Dedication

I dedicate this book to the memory of my precious mother, Geneva Mae Arbeau.

It is also a tribute to my husband, Larry Parker, and my brother, Richard Arbeau. They were my shoulders to lean on and my soft place to fall. They were there when I needed support, advice, and help in caring for my aging and sick mother.

I also must acknowledge the homecare support workers who cared for my mother and were compassionate and understanding when Mum was having an off day.

To my dear friend, Sharon, who filled in the gap for me when homecare cancelled or I couldn't be there. Mum enjoyed Sharon's company and always said, "Sharon and I had so many laughs today. She cracks me up."

Finally, to God, who gave me the strength to care for my Mum for seven years after my Dad passed in 2016.

Mother-daughter moment.

Introduction

My mother, Geneva Mae Arbeau, will always hold a special place in my heart. I loved to listen to her tell stories about when I was a little girl. I knew by her smile and the glow in her eyes that her mind was taking her back to those special moments. She would tell the same stories from time to time.

We lived miles apart for several years, but we always stayed connected through regular phone calls and visits. Family gatherings were important occasions for my parents, siblings, and their families.

When my parents were aging and in poor health, the time came for me to move close to them. My husband and I sold our home on Grand Manan Island and moved back to Fredericton, New Brunswick where my parents lived in May 2016.

My Mum was struggling to care for my father. Dad had suffered three heart attacks, was diabetic, and was failing. He no longer had a valid driver's license and depended on my mother to take over most of the responsibilities he had always looked after. My mother was exhausted, overwhelmed, and tired. She needed help.

I'm the oldest of five children and I have three brothers: one in Miramichi, New Brunswick; one in Quispamsis, New

Brunswick; and one in Goldsboro, North Carolina. We lost our sister Deb to a brain aneurysm in 2009. You can read her story in my first book, *My Sister's Journey from Headache to Heartache*.

It was my time to give back. God placed me in the right place at the right time.

I'm grateful that I was able to see my parents daily and help them with appointments, groceries, cooking, errands, cleaning, lawncare, and anything else they needed. Dad called me the "basket lady," because I was always going to their home with baskets of goodies. I kept Dad well stocked in biscuits! They never had to plan a meal, because they knew I had their weekly meals prepped and in their freezer.

Dad loved his biscuits.

In November 2016, Mum and Dad were both sick in the hospital. Mum had pneumonia and Dad had suffered another heart attack. After ten days in the hospital, my father was moved to the palliative care unit and passed early that evening. Mum released herself against the doctor's wishes.

Thus began my time as Mum's primary caregiver. I did it with love and compassion and fulfilled her needs to the best of my ability. She would look at me with that stern look and say to me, "Remember, I'm the boss." That was her way of telling me that things were to be done her way. Then she would smile or wink at me.

No regrets!

I Can't Breathe

On a cold Sunday evening in December, I made my mother her supper and we settled in for the evening. Mum was snuggled in her recliner with her woolly slippers on her feet and soft pink blanket tucked around her. She asked for her word search book, a cup of tea, and one of my shortbread cookies, which she loved.

When Mum was comfortable, I picked up a book, crawled up onto the bed, fluffed the pillows, and proceeded to allow the pages to take me to another place.

All was quiet as Mum searched for words to circle. Meanwhile, my story was taking me to a faraway place. I was hopeful that it would be a good night.

Crash!

What was happening? I looked at Mum as she threw her word search book on the floor and put her recliner chair in an upright position. She was gasping. Her hands were outreached, like she was clawing for air.

I jumped off the bed and got her inhaler. I then found a cold cloth to wipe the beads of perspiration from her forehead. I put a mask on her face and started the mist machine in hopes that it would help.

As I checked her blood pressure, I was terrified. Then I checked her oxygen level, all the while praying. Finally I phoned 911, for an ambulance to come and help.

At last, I phoned my husband Larry to come to Mum's apartment.

Mum's anxiety wasn't helping, despite my efforts to calm her. Nothing worked. Her breathing was very laboured and she was struggling. Her skin was grey, her lips turning purple.

The fire department responded first and the ambulance arrived shortly after. The paramedics worked on Mum, monitoring her vital signs as well as checking her heart and lungs. They also gave her more inhalers, but nothing helped. The ambulance wasn't equipped with oxygen. Mum needed oxygen.

The ambulance proceeded to take her to the hospital while I assured her that I would be there as soon as I changed from my pjs. I ran up to my apartment, which was only a minute away, and changed and got my coat and boots.

Larry drove me to the hospital where I stayed with Mum in the emergency room for the rest of that evening and overnight.

Mum was admitted, but she remained in the emergency room area for five days due to a lack of beds. She waited on a stretcher in a hallway, close to the nurses' station, for the first two days. They monitored her closely.

Eventually she was moved to a converted conference room with two other patients, in another part of the emergency unit, until a bed became available.

I went home the next morning to get a few things she would need for another brief stay in the hospital, like many times before. I was back within two hours, though, and Mum was still awake, waiting for me. She was afraid to go to sleep.

The doctor and nurses were so kind and caring to my mother. The doctor confirmed that only one of Mum's lungs was working. They did much bloodwork, took urine samples, and ordered x-rays and a variety of tests. The IV pumped fluids into Mum's arm to keep her hydrated. Another bag of fluid entered through a tube, helping her to relax. The oxygen helped regulate her breathing.

On the fifth day, Mum was moved to the third floor. She seemed content as she sat up in a chair, searching for words in her word search book. We chatted and prayed together. I took a few pictures of her, including some of the two of us lying on her bed. I loved capturing this moment on my phone.

"Put that phone away. No more pictures," Mum would say. But then she'd add, "Let me see that picture."

After a short rest, she ate a little supper. I combed her hair, brushed her dentures, and helped her change into a clean nightie, housecoat, and clean fuzzy socks. Mum didn't like the yellow hospital socks and refused to wear them.

My sister told me years ago that I should have been a nurse. Maybe she was right. I do have a caring and compassionate heart.

I got Mum tucked in for the night and prepared to go home.

"Don't leave," Mum said. "You just got here."

Knowing she had been through quite an ordeal, I assured her that I would be back the next morning. Mum just closed her eyes.

I kissed her good night. She seemed okay with me leaving.

I stopped by the nurses' station to advise them that Mum would be asking them to call me if she woke in the night. She had done that every night of every stay in the hospital. Mum didn't like the dark and didn't like to be alone. I also asked the nurse only to call me if it was an emergency, otherwise I would be right there by Mum's side in the morning.

One Day at a Time

As I drove home, I thought of my dear mother lying in the hospital—and I kept thinking about it after I got home and into the late hours.

Whenever I'd seemed upset or anxious about something as a child, my mother had repeated her favourite quote: "Just take it one day at a time." Sometimes she sang it to me.

My mind went back May 2016.

Larry and I had moved back to Fredericton, New Brunswick after living on Grand Manan Island for eighteen years. Mum and Dad had been so happy that we would be living close to them. They arrived at our apartment with fish and chips before we had finished unloading the moving truck.

Mum gave me the biggest hug and whispered in my ear, "My baby girl is back home." Dad gave me a big ole bear hug, too, as tears dripped down our cheeks.

"You two weeping willows, stop that crying," Mum said. "Your food is getting cold."

I knew then that God had placed me in the right place at the right time.

We loved our new place and it was a joy to have my parents dine with us from time to time. Sometimes we took them to Dad's favourite fast food restaurant. Dad loved the burgers and Mum liked the baked potato with sour cream and chives. Mum's preferred fast food was donairs, so on occasion she and I would go out for a donair and take a burger home for Dad.

I was thankful to be there for my parents. I started making meals and treats for them, including biscuits and bread. I carried the goodies to their house in a large basket. Dad and Mum would be standing in their living room window when I drove into the yard.

"There comes the basket lady," Dad would say to Mum. "I wonder what she has for us today." He would greet me at the door with a big smile. "How is the basket lady today?"

As I look back, those were special moments which I will cherish forever.

Dad's body was getting weary. His mind was tired and he struggled to regulate his diabetes. He had fallen a few times, his short-term memory was failing him, and he slept most of the time. Mum was concerned.

I was concerned, too, so I made an appointment with Dad's doctor for a consultation.

On the drive to the doctor's office, Dad told me that he was going to ask for a stronger sleeping pill. I made sure that didn't happen. I spoke to the doctor before Dad went in and advised her what Dad was going to ask for. I told the doctor that my father was already taking way too many pills; if she prescribed more sleeping pills, I wouldn't be getting the prescription filled. She understood.

The doctor gave Dad an extensive checkup and the results of previous tests weren't alarming, especially considering he had already suffered three heart attacks.

Before we left the doctor, she told Dad to take Tylenol for his arthritis, since it could help relieve the pain in his back and chest. She handed me a card with the date for a follow-up appointment the next month.

The summer went by with only a few glitches. We were happy to have homecare for Dad three hours a day. That gave Mum some relief.

Dad wasn't too happy to have a stranger sit with him, though. He said that he wasn't a child and didn't want any stranger to read a book to him about the Miramichi just because he had been born and raised on the Miramichi.

That was the end of storytime for Dad.

As Dad grew too weak to walk far, he also suffered pain in his feet and legs and back. He struggled to stay awake, too. But the most difficult part was that he couldn't go to church.

My father was a retired pastor and loved telling others about God. Even while lying in the hospital after a heart attack, he had been grateful for the opportunity to share about God's love. He didn't have a college education or high school diploma, but he could certainly quote from the Bible. He was self-taught. He was blessed with the gift God had given him.

I became a familiar face at the hospital emergency room that summer between May and November. I was there with Dad because his sugar levels were often too high, probably because he would get up at night to snack on things he shouldn't have. Mum would hear him up, then go out to the kitchen and snap the light on. Mum would ask him what he was doing up in the middle of the night. Was he roaming around in the dark, looking for sweets?

"Oh, I just had a little taste," Dad would say.

Mum would tell him to go back to bed. Dad would just shake his head, roll those big brown eyes, and make his way back to the bedroom.

If I hadn't been at the hospital emergency room with Dad, I would have been there with Mum. She had many allergies and was also asthmatic. So often she panicked while trying to catch her breath. Sometimes taking her inhaler as prescribed, doing her breathing exercises, and breathing into a paper bag didn't work. In those cases, she would head to the emergency room by ambulance with me by her side until the nurses and doctor could get her breathing back to normal. Sometimes it took a few hours and other times she had to stay overnight or even a couple of days. Each time her meds were changed, hoping that the new combination would work.

We coped by taking it all one day at a time and giving thanks for the good times. We asked God for strength to get us through the rough days.

Last Call

My Dad's last call came in the early evening. Mum was struggling to breathe and he needed me to get there quickly. He was afraid and Mum was in panic mode. Meanwhile, Dad himself was sick with a cold and suffering from chest and back pain.

I called the ambulance and met the paramedics at my parents' home. Mum was assessed and taken to the hospital, but the paramedics recommended that my father call an ambulance for himself. He assured them that he would be fine after he'd gotten a good rest.

I followed behind the ambulance. After a few hours, Mum was admitted to the hospital with pneumonia.

Daylight was just breaking, so I decided to go home and get my mother some personal items and check on my father. I packed a few items for Mum's stay in the hospital.

I found that Dad was still sleeping, but after taking one look at him I realized that he needed to be checked as well.

When I woke him, gently, he had a high fever and was coughing nonstop. He held his chest while continuing to cough. I washed him as best I could and got him dressed. He was insistent that I take him to the hospital, though. I was not to call an ambulance. I obliged him, with great anxiousness, and got him in the car.

As I drove, Dad was coughing and holding his chest. I prayed for God to get me to the hospital safely.

"Dad, don't you dare die on me," I blurted aloud.

He didn't say a word. He just looked at me and rolled his eyes. Dad was a man of few words, but his expressions told a person exactly what he was thinking.

I parked at the entrance of the emergency room, then ran in and asked for help. The attendants came with a wheelchair and wheeled Dad inside. I told them that my father had suffered three heart attacks in the past and I thought he may be having another one. I also told them he might have pneumonia.

Dad was assessed immediately.

After some time had passed, the on-call doctor that morning asked to speak to me privately. The news was devastating. Dad had suffered another heart attack. He also had pneumonia, a collapsed lung, and his kidneys were failing. It was much more than arthritis in his chest and back.

Dad was moved to the ICU.

Watching the nurses work on Dad gave me a glimmer of hope. He was hooked up to monitors, beeping and squealing. He had a pole above his bed with several bags of fluids being pumped into his body.

As the nurses monitored Dad, I went to the next floor of the hospital where Mum was staying. When I updated her on what had happened, she was distraught, but she was confined to bed and couldn't see Dad.

I stayed with him day and night and went back to visit Mum from time to time each day. I also went home for an hour or so when a visitor came to visit my father. It gave me a chance to shower and change my clothes before heading right back to the hospital.

On day five, the nurses helped me get Mum into a wheelchair. I took her to see Dad. It was a bittersweet reunion.

When Dad saw Mum being wheeled into his room, he smiled and said, "There's my sweetie."

I used my phone to capture their conversation. They held hands and talked for a brief time before Dad fell asleep.

Mum started showing signs of improvement after three or four days and I was able to take her in a wheelchair to visit Dad a few more times.

By day seven, though, Dad was failing quickly. He refused ice cream when I put it to his lips. He refused water on a sponge.

Soon the doctor told me that they couldn't do anything more for him. All the tubes were removed and the monitors wheeled from his room. Dad slept.

I updated my brothers and asked them to contact the rest of our family. All I could do was watch Dad sleep and pray that God would give us strength to get through the heartbreak.

I held Dad's hand as he laid in bed with his eyes closed. I'm not much of a singer, but I sang songs I had learned in Sunday school and church. I read to him from his Bible daily. I'll never know whether he heard me, but I hope it was a comfort to him.

I also had brief visits with Mum, but I didn't give her any details on Dad's condition. Other family members went to be with Mum while I stayed with Dad.

On the ninth day, Dad opened his eyes and looked at me.

"You're still here," he said. "I need to ask a favour of you."

"Sure. What can I do, Dad?"

"Will you look after Mum when I'm gone?"

I promised I would.

Those were the last words Dad spoke to me.

On the evening of the tenth day, he was moved to palliative care. I was joined around Dad's bed by my cousin Donnie and my nephew Troy and his wife.

My father was only in the palliative care unit for a brief time. He took a few deep breaths, then one last breath, and at last his spirit left the room. Dad's lifeless body lay on the freshly made bed just for him.

We said our goodbyes. I kissed my father for the last time, then gathered up his personal belongings and went to break the dreaded news to Mum.

Mum later told me that when she saw us coming towards her, she knew Dad was gone.

His earthly journey ended on November 14, 2016.

Mum signed herself out of the hospital the next day, against her doctor's wishes. She was a strong-willed lady and she was determined to go home.

In Memory of My Dad

Rev. Willis Arbeau
1928–2016

I fall down
When darkness overcomes me
And sadness steals my joy
With wounded heart and tear-stained face
I know just what to do

I fall down
I fall down on my knees and praise him
I fall down
I fall down on my knees and thank him
For the life he has given me

When sorrow brings me heartache
And life seems so unfair
Cause my Dad is no longer there
To love me and help me share a prayer

I know just what to do
I fall down
I fall down on my knees and thank him
I fall down
I fall down on my knees and praise him
For the life he has given me

You see, my Daddy was a preacher man
He was a man of prayer
He has now gone on to his reward
To that mansion in the sky
And left me with a prayer

I fall down
I fall down on my knees and praise him
I fall down
I fall down on my knees and thank him
For the life he has given me

When blessings fall
And joy abounds
And I feel God's loving touch
I know just what to do

I fall down
I fall down on my knees and praise him
I fall down
I fall down on my knees and thank him
For giving me a loving Dad
Who taught me how to pray

My dad.

What About Mum

When the funeral was over, the family made their way, one by one, from the gravesite to my parents' home. There was a great assortment of food and refreshments for everyone to enjoy. It was calming to listen to so many people express their special memories of my father and watch Mum's reaction as the conversations flowed throughout the day.

Evening dawned, friends left, and family went their separate ways. Some had to catch flights while others had a long drive home. My brother Jerry and his wife Christine stayed with Mum that night.

The following day brought many changes. My mother wasn't doing so well. Her anxiety was affecting her breathing and she was afraid to be alone. She was confused and cried so much. She was sick to her stomach. Reality was setting in that Dad was gone.

Mum reached out for a hug. "Barb, please don't you leave me."

I promised I would stay with her.

My mind flashed back to that final moment with Dad when he'd had asked me to look after Mum when he was gone.

I kept my promise. That was the day I became my mother's primary caregiver. I was fortunate to have homecare support three hours every day during the week. That gave me a little time to go to my apartment, check on my husband, and make him a meal or pick up a few groceries. Or I could use the time to pick up Mum's prescriptions. It was hectic, but I had a promise to keep. No matter how rough things got, I had to push through.

My brother Richard drove from Quispamsis a few times and stayed with Mum for a night during the weekend. That gave me a little time to be home with my husband.

I'm so thankful and blessed that my husband, Larry, was so understanding and supportive while I cared for Mum.

I chuckle now to think back to that winter when I stayed with Mum at her house. I think—no, I know—it was one of the worst winters I ever experienced. It snowed too much and I had to shovel the walkway and path up the driveway for the homecare worker before ten o'clock every morning. Mum would stand in the living room window as I shovelled, prayed, cried, and kept shovelling until the job was finished. I was angry at God for taking my father. I was angry at my brothers for not being there. I was a mess for a while.

One stormy morning while shovelling the walk, I spotted a small snowplough driving down the street. Mum knocked on the window and pointed at the plough.

I took off, trying to run through the deep snow, falling and losing my boot in the snowdrift. I left the boot and got to the middle of the street, wearing only one boot, and waved my arms in the air like a wild person. I hoped the plough driver would see me through the heavy snow.

He did see me and stopped. I hired him to plough the yard and walk, all while Mum kept standing in the window. She clapped her hands when she saw the plough push the bucket of snow towards me; right on top of the snow was my boot! I tipped the driver and thanked him for saving the day.

It was one of my duties to carry in wood to fill the wood box by the little stove in the downstairs family room. It was too cold outside and the wood was heavy. I would cry while doing this, crying more. I cried a lot that winter. Some may say I had the winter blues.

I found a contact on social media who came and cleared the snow off the roof and cleared the back deck. I wasn't brave or foolish enough to tackle either of those jobs.

The good days outweighed the bad days, however, and Mum and I got through it.

We didn't celebrate much that Christmas. I decorated a little tree and put it in the window, next to a picture of my dad and my sister.

Mum and I were still trying to find our new normal. We were a team, and we were tough old birds.

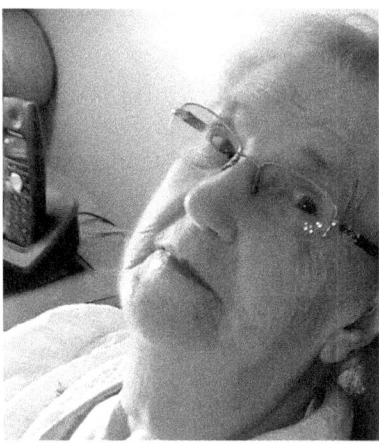

My mum.

Five

Yellow Socks and Purple Onions

Mum began to feel better. She was eating and sleeping more reliably. But then she came down with a bad cold, with fever, chills, and body aches.

Her go-to treatment for a cold was a vapour rub and medicated ointment. Close to bedtime, she put the vapour rub up around her nose and put ointment on her chest. She also pressed a towel across her chest and neck. Then she put on her flowered nightcap to keep her curls in place.

I couldn't stop laughing. Mum got a little upset because I couldn't hold it together long enough to tell her what was so funny.

When I pointed to the mirror, she saw her reflection and realized why I was laughing. We had a great laugh together. Belly laughs are good for the soul.

Mum mentioned that she had read in a magazine about a different kind of treatment: putting sliced purple onions on the bottom of one's feet and wearing socks to bed. It was supposed to clear your cold.

Well, I pulled on some clothes over my pjs and went to the corner store, minutes away. Lucky for me, they had two purple onions.

I was back at the house within ten minutes. I sliced the onions and pulled out some yellow socks, the ones a person wears when they're in the hospital.

At first Mum was a bit reluctant, but she agreed that it was worth a try. She allowed me to get the yellow socks on. I then tucked the onion slices on the bottoms of both her feet.

Mum insisted that I sleep with her. It was a race to see who could get to sleep first, since we both snored. We were so stressed and tired those days, but we managed to sleep a few hours. On a few occasions, Mum would give me a poke and tell me to turn over.

Some mornings, Mum would wake and wonder where I'd gone. She would find me sleeping on the sofa. When she snored, I knew she was having a good sleep. Not wanting to wake her, I'd grab my pillow and a blanket and go quietly to the living room.

The morning after the onion foot treatment, light shone through the bedroom window. But we awoke to a smell I cannot even describe.

"Get those socks and onions off my feet right now!" Mum insisted.

The socks and onions went straight into the trash. Then we removed the bedding and threw it in the washer. The mattress had to be aired out that day, so we opened the bedroom window wide.

Mum also insisted that I soak her feet to get rid of the stink. I added a little body wash, some mouthwash, and a squirt of dish detergent to the warm water. She soaked her feet until the water was cool, which did help the smell to dissipate.

I am sad to report that the onions did not cure her cold.

When I look back at some of the adventures we had, the laughs and tears we shared, and the stories she told me about my childhood and her years raising children while Dad worked… well, I get a warm, fuzzy feeling of Mum's love.

Some nights we stayed up too late talking. I got to know my mother in a new way. We formed a real mother-daughter bond, something I had wanted for years.

In my teen years, Mum had been so busy raising my siblings that we hadn't been able to form a close relationship. I knew she loved me, though, and that she was always there when I needed her.

In those years, she worked in the evenings, cleaning offices with her friend Luella while I cared for the younger ones. I'm remarkably close to my two younger brothers.

One evening when I wanted to go out with friends, Mum told me I couldn't because I had to babysit. I exploded at her and told her I was tired of being her built-in babysitter.

I regret those words today.

Mum explained that she had to work to help provide for our family. I never complained about babysitting after that. I apologized. I still remember the big hug my mother gave me.

While taking care of her after Dad's passing, I knew I was in the right place at the right time. The memories we made were priceless.

Six
The Fall

Mum finally recovered from the cold, but she was still weak and unsteady when she walked. She had been through so much. With her being sick and me being so occupied with caring for her—including shovelling snow, carrying wood, making meals for both Mum and my husband—I don't think either of us took the time to grieve. We were in survival mode.

I asked Mum not to go downstairs to the family room unless I was with her. I was afraid she would slip on the wooden stairs or trip on her long housecoat. She agreed that we would only go there together. Sometimes we wanted to sit by the cozy fire and have a cup of tea and chat while looking at the pictures she kept in a large wooden chest at the end of the sofa.

One day, I left Mum in the care of the homecare worker while I went to pick up groceries and prescriptions. I also went home to check on my husband, who wasn't feeling well.

I got back to Mum's house just before one o'clock and didn't see the caregiver's car in the driveway. My first thought was that something bad had happened and no one had called me.

I ran into the house, went into the bedroom, and called out to Mum. No answer. Then I ran downstairs. Mum was lying on the floor just inches from the woodstove. The caregiver was nowhere in sight.

I screamed, thinking Mum was dead. I got down on the floor beside her and realized she was still breathing. When I shook her, she opened her eyes and looked at me. I checked her over for broken bones.

"Help me up," she said.

I got her up off the floor and sat her in the recliner. I asked her where the caregiver was.

"She was coughing, so I sent her home," she explained. "I didn't want to get another cold."

"But what in the world were you doing downstairs when we agreed you wouldn't come down here?"

Mum looked at me with tears in her eyes. "I just wanted to sit in your father's chair by the fire."

It turned out that she had sat there for a brief time, had a short nap, and then decided to go back upstairs before I came home. But she got up from the chair, she felt dizzy and tried to sit back down…

That was all she could recall—that is, until she opened her eyes to see me staring down at her.

I didn't have the heart to scold her. Instead we cuddled up in Dad's chair by the fire and cried. We cuddled, rocked in the chair, and reminisced about Dad and how much we missed him. After a little while, we dried our eyes and I helped Mum up the steps. She told me that she was sorry for scaring me.

We never mentioned it again. I felt her pain and sorrow over missing Dad.

My mother was an incredibly determined woman. If she wanted to do something, she was going to try her best to do it on her own.

We had our moments. Mum thought I was overprotective, but she knew I was only trying to care for her. On more than one occasion, she reminded me that she was still the boss. That made me chuckle. She was struggling with her health, her loss of Dad, and dealing with either me or the homecare worker being around. If we thought she was in the bathroom too long, one of us would knock on the door to ensure she was okay. That drove Mum crazy.

"I can't even go to the bathroom in peace," she would say.

We tried to joke about this, but I knew Mum was serious about her frustration.

Seven

Time for a Change

After three months, it was time to think about making some changes to Mum's care. She made it clear that she wasn't going to stay in the house by herself.

After discussing the situation with my brothers and considering all the options, it was decided to put the house up for sale and try to find a small apartment for Mum, somewhere close to where I lived.

An apartment soon became available in the same complex where Larry and I lived. Some would say it was luck, but I call it a God thing.

I took Mum to view the apartment and she was so pleased with it. She was happy that she would be so close but still have a place to call her own. She also felt relieved that it was a secure building, because she was nervous about being alone at night.

We put the house on the market and placed a deposit to hold the apartment.

I had to give the tenant in the downstairs apartment of my parents' split-level home notice to move, as the house was for sale. I also had to prepare the house for the realtor to show to potential buyers.

When I knocked on the downstairs apartment door, I almost fell over from the rotten smell. I had noticed this nauseating scent before without being able to find the source. Now I knew where it was coming from.

The tenant opened the door and I covered my nose. I handed over the paper notice.

As soon as the tenant had moved out, I prepared to go inside the empty apartment. What was I getting myself into?

I put on some coveralls hanging in the downstairs storage room. I double-masked, double-gloved, and took the plunge.

The apartment was a disaster area. I used a shovel and a broom to clear the trash and spilled food and rotten eggs from the floors. I then sprayed the oven, cleaned the fridge, and cleaned and cleaned and cleaned.

It took several days of cleaning, carpet shampooing, disinfecting, painting, and making repairs. Between my brother Richard and I, we got the apartment back to its original state.

By the time the house sold, the apartment was ready. Mum was doing much better.

The time had come to go through my parents' things. I sorted, purged, and listed items for sale on social media. I packed for days, filling the car and taking boxes over to the apartment whenever the homecare worker arrived to be with Mum. A few times, Richard came with his larger vehicle and took pictures, mirrors, and small tables and lamps and whatever else would fit.

We hired a moving company to take the large furniture. While this was going on, I took Mum to our apartment where Larry entertained her—or perhaps she was the one to entertain him. At least I knew she was well cared for while Richard and I finished setting up her new apartment.

Soon everything was done. The curtains were hung, pictures placed on the wall, beds were made, and dishes put away in the cupboard. Even the tea and cookies were ready when Larry brought Mum down in the elevator to her new home.

Mum was all smiles when she stepped inside. She was so happy, and we were so happy that she was happy.

She was surprised to see everything was unpacked and put in place. I even had her dishes in the right order in her buffet. I never did tell her my method: I'd taken a picture of how she had them arranged before packing up. Then I referred to the picture when setting things up again.

We were a happy bunch as we had our first cup of tea in Mum's new home.

Eight

Fitting In

Richard spent the first night with Mum in her new apartment and I slept in my own bed.

Now that Mum was feeling better, we had many appointments. First were her breathing tests, to see whether the inhalers she was using needed to be changed. Then we went to see her eye doctor, who gave her a new prescription. A few weeks later, we had to get her hearing checked, too. It turned out she needed new hearing aids. Well, we went to a new store—and she wasn't at all happy with the ones they gave her. She got a refund and we went to another place in town. Only then was Mum pleased.

I'm not sure what Mum and I enjoyed most; was it the satisfaction of keeping all these appointments and having satisfactory results or was it the great social outings we enjoyed as we went to various restaurants around the city? We just enjoyed being out in the nice weather after the hectic winter. And whenever we went out, we usually met someone Mum knew. It was wonderful to watch her chat with her friends and see a smile on her face.

Mum liked to browse through dollar stores, browse the aisles of the department stores nearby, and walk through the mall. We frequently took short breaks while out so she could catch her breath and rest.

"I'm all out of puff," she would say. "I need to sit for a bit."

I took pictures wherever we went and posted them on social media. Some of the pictures showed us with funny hats. Others had us posing with a clown who made balloon figures for Mum. We took photos at the local coffee shop, too, and some with our homemade Easter bonnets. Then there were the family gatherings, birthday parties, and socials. There are videos of Mum knitting, too. It was just Mum being Mum.

The most cherished pictures are the ones I have of Mum and Dad renewing their vows and the ones of Mum reading her Bible. She read her Bible every morning when she got up and every evening before she went to bed. If she wasn't feeling well, she'd make sure her Bible was nearby so she could read a verse or two from time to time. I'm so thankful for having Christian parents who read the Bible to me and my siblings and prayed with us and for us daily.

My mother loved her cozy and inviting apartment. She had a splendid view of people coming and going and I was only a minute away. She continued to have homecare three hours per day, from ten o'clock in the morning until one o'clock in the afternoon. The rest of the time, I filled in the hours. She always had a puzzle set up on her dining room table to work on and she thoroughly enjoyed her word search books. I bought her a tablet and showed her how to use it. She enjoyed browsing through social media. She was pleased to be able to watch church services since she couldn't physically get out to church very often anymore.

From time to time, friends from Mum's church came to visit, which surely gave her a lift. She also enjoyed visits from her longtime friend Vera, and Vera's daughter Valerie. There was also our friend and neighbour, Sharon, and another dear friend, Pam, in addition to many others.

Mum loved to have flowers on her deck in the summer. My brother Jerry and his wife Christine always brought beautiful hanging baskets for Mum's birthday and Mother's Day. As soon as I hung the pots on her deck, Mum would say, "Now take a picture of my beautiful flowers and post it on Facebook." And I would.

She reminded me daily to water her plants and keep them looking just so. She insisted that I find her a pretty hummingbird feeder. I did. She genuinely enjoyed watching the sweet little birds flutter around her plants and drink from the feeder. I took many pictures of her beautiful flowers and the hummingbirds and posted them just like she asked me to.

As long as I can remember, Mum loved to decorate. Due to her allergies, she wasn't able to work outside or be around flowers. Between me and her homemakers, we kept her flowers and hummingbird feeder well maintained. I got her a lighted tree for her deck, which she also loved.

She then had the idea that she needed colourful birds on the tree. Off to the dollar store I went, where I bought little birds with clips and attached them to the tree. Pretty things made her happy and that was my goal. I wanted to make her happy and have her enjoy every day.

Mum loved the sound of chimes blowing in the wind. Jerry and Christine bought her a beautiful chime which I hung from the ceiling of her deck. Many people complimented her decorated deck. I had the lighted tree on a timer so it came on at 7:00 p.m. and turned off at 10:00 p.m. each evening.

Power outages sometimes messed up the timer, though.

We once got a notice from the landlord saying that a neighbour had complained that the lights from the tree were shining in their bedroom window. I checked the timer and confirmed that it was still set from 7:00–10:00 p.m.

Mum was irritated and wanted to know who was complaining. She wanted to tell them to close their window blind. Instead we just unplugged the tree.

A couple of months later, we received a general notice that all tenants had to remove the chimes from their decks, again due to complaints. Mum was really aggravated and told me that she wanted to move. She wasn't used to apartment living. This was just another hurdle, but we got through it after some time.

Some of the other women in the building would drop by to visit and introduce themselves. Mum became friends with several of them. They gathered in the social room and chatted, working on puzzles during the afternoons and early evenings. Mum always had my phone number tucked in her pocket in case she needed me. I wanted her to have her freedom, but I also wanted her to know that I was just a phone call away.

I was sure to tuck Mum in every night and make sure all the appliances were turned off. It was important to ensure she had everything she needed right by her bedside.

This worked for a few weeks, until Mum had a flare up with her breathing again. She phoned me in the middle of the night and I ran down the stairs to her apartment. That night, I had to call the ambulance. This was her first trip to the hospital from her new apartment.

I followed behind the ambulance and we spent the night in the emergency room, only coming home late the next day with prescriptions for more medications. The doctors gave us an "action plan" to put into effect when Mum experienced a COPD flare up.

What was COPD? I had thought she just had allergies and asthma. Mum had been dealing with this most of her life.

We had lived for a time in McAdam, New Brunswick, a railway town that had trains coming and going every day. The fumes from those trains had really affected Mum's breathing and she had gone to the hospital on numerous occasions due to breathing issues and pneumonia. She always told us that the smell of diesel fuel bothered her lungs.

When my parents lived in Caribou, Maine, her health seemed to improve.

After that, thought, when my parents lived in Edmundston, New Brunswick, Mum complained about the smoke coming from the nearby mill.

"It really chokes me and makes it hard for me to breath," she'd say.

I never knew she had chronic obstructive pulmonary disease! So after we were told this at the hospital, I immediately called Mum's family doctor and got an appointment for two weeks later.

Maybe Mum had known about this diagnosis and never told us. One day, I asked her about it.

"I don't want to talk about it," she said.

We will never know.

At times she would lose her voice, or she would only be able to speak in a low whisper. I assumed this was due to her allergies, but I now wanted to have it checked out. Mum was great at looking after others, but she never took the time to properly care for herself.

When the day came to see the family doctor, we went in together. He was such a wonderful doctor to my mother. I had so many questions and he educated me about what had happened in Mum's lungs.

She did indeed have COPD. In fact, the disease was in its final stage.

We also discussed my concerns about Mum's faint voice.

The doctor arranged an appointment with a throat specialist. After viewing the scans, X-rays, and test results, we learned that the problem was too risky to try to fix. Her vocal cords had been damaged from a previous procedure when she'd had her esophagus stretched.

Obviously Mum hadn't shared everything about her health with me, but now I was making it my business to care for her and help her to the best of my ability. Some might have called this being controlling, but I called it love and compassion. I was keeping the promise I had made to my father.

The days were getting longer and Mum was doing well, considering her health issues.

Her eighty-seventh birthday was coming up on April 1 and I planned a surprise birthday party for her in the social room. I invited family, close friends, and delivered an open invitation to the tenants of our building.

The homecare worker assured me that she would keep Mum in her apartment that morning while I set the social room up with all the goodies and decorations for the planned surprise. I thought it would be a clever way for Mum to meet her neighbours, having forgotten that Mum could see people coming and going from her living room window.

When everything was in order, I went to pick up Mum and bring her to the social room. But no way was she leaving her apartment. She had seen some of her friends and family walking in and they hadn't come over to her place.

"I know you're up to something," she said, "and I'm not leaving this apartment."

After some coaxing and threatening to put her in a wheelchair and wheel her out, she gave in. She was indeed surprised to see so many of her friends, family, and tenants as they sang Happy Birthday to her. She sat in her decorated chair and had the time of her life.

I didn't throw any more surprise birthday parties for her, but we did celebrate each of her birthdays with a drop-in invitation to friends, family, and tenants. Mum enjoyed these visits and conversations. She would make sure I served each person a piece of her birthday cake and ice cream and glass of her favourite punch.

Mum would enjoy reading all the cards when the celebration was over. She'd talk about her party for days after it was over.

Mum loved tea socials. A few times, she mentioned that she'd like to invite a few friends for tea. I baked fancy cookies or squares and prepared a nice display with her teacups and saucers, a pretty tablecloth, and napkins. That way, Mum and a few ladies could enjoy afternoon tea.

On the second Tuesday of each month, the tenants of our building gathered for a potluck supper. I always made two dishes: a dinner dish and a dessert. Mum would get the fancy place settings from the dining room buffet, for both me and her, and we'd take them out to the social room to hold our place at the table.

Mum enjoyed the first couple of years in this apartment. I tried to keep her active when she felt well, and other days we just go for a drive.

On one occasion we drove up to Durham. She wanted to show me where she had lived with her grandparents as a child. There were many off-roads in the area and I took a wrong turn at one point.

"I think we're lost," Mum said.

We backtracked and had to stop at a garage and ask directions. We were lost! We didn't drive on unfamiliar roads after that, and we never did find the homestead we had been looking for.

I thought Mum was doing much better.

That's when she started phoning me in the middle of the night. She was afraid and thought people were trying to get into her apartment. She couldn't breathe good and needed me.

Those calls continued over time and I spent many nights lying beside her, trying to calm and reassure her. I prayed for God's help.

During the daytime, Mum seemed okay. The homecare ladies kept her company, worked on puzzles with her, helped her find words in her word search book, enjoyed tea and snacks with her. They also listened as Mum told them stories while browsing through Mum's photos.

As nighttime approached, though, it seemed like Mum's anxiety overwhelmed her. The fear of being alone was too much for her.

One night, in particular, Mum phoned me in a panic. She told me that Dad was there standing in the bedroom door. She said that he spoke to her and asked if she was going to sleep all day.

"Barb, hurry!" she said to me. "Come and see him. He looks just like he did before he died."

When I got there, Mum was crying. She was scared and confused. I held her in my arms and laid beside her for the rest of the night. I tried to assure her that it must have been a dream, but she was sure it had been real.

Maybe it was.

I was feeling sleep-deprived and concerned. I applied for more homecare hours and thankfully my request was approved.

My brother and I refer to these as "God things." We experienced many "God things" through blessings, answered prayers, and healing.

With extended hours of care for Mum during the day, I hired private care to stay a couple of nights during the week. Mum was okay as long as someone was with her. I depended on this help and Mum enjoyed these people's company. I'm so grateful for the opportunity to meet so many kind and caring people during these years.

Mum reading her Bible.

Nine

The Flu

Early in the evening on Saturday, April 8, 2017, I was in the kitchen making chicken soup. My mother and my husband were showing signs of having the flu and I thought chicken soup might help. At least I'd always heard that chicken soup was the thing to make for someone who felt ill.

I heard a loud thump and ran to the living room. My husband had tried to get up from the sofa and fallen to the floor. He couldn't get up and my first thought was that he'd suffered a stroke.

After several tries, I got him back up on the sofa. I turned the stove burner off and ran to tell Mum what had happened. I also phoned a friend to go stay with Mum.

Larry was rushed to the hospital. In the emergency room, we were told that Larry had suffered a stroke and he was admitted and moved to a semi-private room.

Doctors and nurses crowded around Larry's bed as many tests were conducted. The staff was puzzled. One of the nurses suggested doing a flu swab, and the results showed that Larry had Influenza B. Then Larry was rushed off to another room and put in isolation. Only immediate family could visit, and only when fully clothed in gowns, mask, and gloves.

Something wasn't adding up. When a person suffered a stroke, it usually affected one side of the body. But Larry was paralyzed from the neck down. His eye drooped, his mouth twisted, and the paralysis affected both sides.

The neurologist put on Larry's case ordered a lumbar puncture. After the results came in, the neurologist took me aside and explained that my husband had Miller Fisher syndrome, which is in the same family of diseases as Guillain-Barré syndrome. The body's immune system was damaging the nerves, causing muscle weakness and paralysis.

She didn't give me much hope. In fact, she told me to prepare to have Larry spend the rest of his life in a rehab centre or nursing home.

I was in shock. I was so scared. My whole body shook and I felt like I was going to faint.

As we continued talking, I told her that we served a God who performed miracles. I believed Larry would walk out of the hospital and go back to living in our apartment, not a nursing home or rehab centre.

She looked at me and said, "I hope you're right."

Later that day, the neurologist told us that she knew of a treatment that might help Larry if he was willing to try. It was called intravenous immunoglobin (IVIG).

He agreed. The treatment was ordered and started on day five of his stay.

During the treatment, nurses stayed with him to watch for any signs of rejection. They also took his vital signs every fifteen to thirty minutes.

I went home late that evening to check on Mum and sleep for a few hours. Many people were praying for a miracle.

When I walked into Larry's hospital room the next morning, I couldn't believe what I saw. He was sitting in a chair beside his bed. His droopy eye had corrected itself and his mouth was less twisted. He could even move his fingers.

The isolation ban was lifted and Larry moved back into a semi-private room.

Larry received five IVIG treatments, and with each one his mobility was being restored. The treatment caused Larry to feel very tired, but he was determined to walk again.

By the seventh day, Larry was walking with a walker. By the eighth day, Easter Sunday, he even walked without a walker. He was feeling and looking so much better.

The neurologist went in to see him and reacted in disbelief to the progress he'd made.

"I guess you were right," she said to me. She called him the Miracle Man.

I was able to take the Miracle Man home on April 15. His stay in the hospital had lasted ten long days.

Larry had many scheduled appointments and different reactions to medications after he was released from the hospital, but God answered our prayers. For that, we were so thankful. The outcome could have been much worse.

Larry still has health issues related to this disease, and we continue to take it one day at a time.

Ten

Too Old for Surgery?

On a beautiful and sunny Saturday morning, I dropped Mum at a local hotel to attend a ladies retreat. She looked so nice all dressed up, her hair fixed just the way she liked it. She was anxious to spend time with friends she hadn't seen for a long time. She reminded me what time I should pick her up later that afternoon. I assured her that I would be on time.

Shortly before noon, I received a phone call from one of Mum's friends. She was in a panic and needed me to come back. Mum wasn't feeling well.

Thinking it was another COPD attack, I arrived to find her crying and bent over in pain. Two women helped me get Mum in my car so I could take her to the emergency room.

Thinking back on it later, I don't know why I didn't call an ambulance.

She was admitted and was scheduled for emergency surgery as soon as an operating room became available. Her gallbladder had to be removed. The ultrasound showed that her gallbladder had decayed.

The doctor asked me to call the rest of the family to make them aware of what was happening. He was unsure whether Mum would survive the operation.

The surgery to remove the gallbladder was done at night and Mum came through like a trooper. We were thankful and the doctors were amazed.

Afterward, she wanted a telephone hooked up in her room. That was a big mistake on my part. Mum called me all hours of the night, wanting me to go and sit with her. She was afraid and seemed to forget that I had been with her most of the day. She was confused and I was stressed.

I had to have the phone disconnected, which really upset my mother.

The next morning when I went to visit her, she tried to be mad at me and didn't respond to my questions. That didn't last long, though. I gave her a hug and kiss and told her that I would be back when she wanted to have a visitor.

"Don't you dare leave," she said. "You sit right down in that chair."

So I did what I was told.

Later that day, other family members came to visit and the air cleared. Mum forgot that she was mad. She loved having her family with her.

We got over that hurdle and after two weeks I took her home.

Mum's balance and mobility was declining and her doctor recommended that I get a walker for her. Against her wishes, I did just that. She refused to use it for some time, until she fell and cut her leg and had to have the ambulance take her to the hospital for stitches.

"Well, get me that stupid walker from the storage room," she said when she got home from the hospital. "I don't like it, but it could save me from another fall."

She used the walker from that day onward and was glad to have it for support.

I can't count the number of times the ambulance was called to Mum's apartment. Most of the paramedics knew her by name and they usually took her to the emergency room.

COPD robbed my mother of her breath, and it was so scary to watch the fear in her eyes while she struggled to breathe.

With the help of Mum's family doctor, we were able to get more homecare hours, assistance on a regular basis, and a foot-care lady. I continued to make all her meals, pay her monthly bills, get her groceries and prescriptions, and look after her personal needs. I was thankful for the extra support.

But those phone calls in the middle of the night continued and I kept running to her side to help when I could. If I couldn't help, I would have to call 911.

Eleven

The Broken Chair

Mum came home from the hospital after another COPD flare up. The oxygen she was given helped and we started her on another "action plan" of prednisone and an antibiotic. She breathed better and the prednisone seemed to boost her energy.

For the five days she was on prednisone, she kept me and the homecare girls busy. One day she wanted the living room ornaments all washed and rearranged; there were many of them. Another day she wanted the curtains taken down and washed and the windows cleaned to a sparkling shine. Another day she wanted the fridge cleaned inside and out or the dishes taken out of her buffet and washed and rearranged. These tasks were done on a regular basis, but when Mum made a request, we obliged her. It gave us a chuckle and it gave Mum the feeling of control. We enjoyed making her happy.

For as long as I can remember, Mum kept her home immaculate. When my sister Deb and I were old enough to clean,

Mum showed us the ropes. If we didn't do a job to her expectation, she would send us back to do it again, until she approved.

As children, Deb and I had many arguments over which chores we would do every Saturday before being allowed to go outside. I still have a scar in my right eyebrow where Deb threw a wax can at me. I had been assigned to put the first coat of hard paste wax on the dining room floor, then let it dry until Deb could apply the second coat. When it was Deb's turn to get down on her knees and start waxing, I told her I was going outside while she finished the job.

"Oh no you are not," she said. "You're going to help me wax this stupid floor."

That was all I could remember—until I opened my eyes to see my mother and our neighbour standing over me and my sister bawling her eyes out. She never threw another wax can at me after that.

I miss my sister and hold many fond memories tucked away in my heart.

I remember grumbling when I had to do household chores and help with the kids. As I grew older and had my own home, I'm so thankful that my mother taught me so much. She taught me how to cook, clean, care for children, and make a house a home. Not only was she my mother, she was also my teacher and dearest friend. To this day, I love browsing through her cookbooks and written recipes.

Life was good. Mum felt upbeat. The sun shone.

Mum decided to sit on her deck after her homecare worker left. Remember that her deck faced the front of the building, where people came to the front door to ring the buzzer.

My phone rang. It was someone buzzing to get in.

"Your mother needs you," said the voice on the other end of the line.

It turned out that Mum had seen a stranger walking into the building, and she'd asked him to buzz my number for help. I ran down the steps, entered Mum's apartment, and called her name. I could hear her, but I couldn't see her.

That's when I noticed that the patio door was open. There she was on the deck, her arms and feet pointed up in the air while her bottom sat on the floor. She had fallen through the cloth lawnchair!

With the help of a neighbour, we got her out of the tangled mess. I was sure she would have broken bones, but she didn't have a scratch. She never went out on her deck again.

That summer, my husband had to be admitted to the hospital twice. The first time it was for kidney stone surgery. The second time, he was diagnosed with pericarditis.

I had to do a juggling act, often needing to be in two places at the same time. With the help of homecare workers and private care for Mum, we managed to survive the many bumps during this season of our lives.

When I wasn't with my mother, she was always on my mind. When I heard a siren, my heart leaped and I sprang into action. I always thought the worst and I had to see for myself that Mum was okay. In fact, I never went anywhere without my phone. I lived in fear, worrying that Mum might fall, which she did several times. It was exceedingly difficult to watch the changes in her from day to day, month to month, and year to year.

Mum and I talked about getting old. She told me that she didn't feel her age. She said that she still had the desire to cook, clean, decorate, prepare meals, and do all the other things she excelled at. But that's all it was—a desire. She knew she wasn't physically capable of doing any of these tasks she had once done with pride and perfection.

At times she tried to assist me with baking, preparing strawberries to make freezer jam, cutting up apples to make applesauce, and slicing up onions and cucumbers to make pickles. I so enjoyed having her in the kitchen with me. I wanted her to feel needed and appreciated. She couldn't stand for more than a few minutes before having to sit down, which was frustrating for her.

Mum had always enjoyed decorating her home for special occasions and I tried to continue that tradition after she moved to her apartment. She had boxes of decorations for all occasions.

A week or so before Easter, she would remind me that it was time to get her Easter decorations up. I hung colourful plastic Easter eggs on her lighted tree on the deck. Her patio door window displayed hanging Easter bunnies and her living room tables and fireplace were adorned with decorations. Her beautiful lily, which I got for her each Easter, formed the centrepiece on her dining room table.

When Mum moved to the apartment, she got reacquainted with a friend from long ago. The first Easter in her new home, she and I got together with this friend, Gladys, and made Easter bonnets to hang on our door. It's a precious memory.

I followed tradition and made the big Easter dinner, like Mum had always done.

"Remember to make extra," she said. "You never know who might show up."

I obliged her. If we had leftovers, that was okay. I treated the neighbours and Mum could have a reheated dinner the following day.

In mid-January, Mum would get anxious to display her Valentine decorations. She would stand by the patio door window and watch me hang the red decorations on the tree on her deck. Then she'd sit in her chair and tell me what she would like to have hung in her patio door window, and where to put a few decorations on her fireplace and end tables. She always had a decoration of some sort on her patio door window. If she wasn't displaying special occasion decorations, she had me hang her beautiful stained-glass ornaments with suction cup hooks. She had many of them and all were gifts from friends and family.

By the first week of November, I was digging out the boxes of Christmas decorations. Mum had so many beautiful ornaments. I hung the garland and Christmas lights on her deck before the weather got too cold. Mum insisted that I turn them on after I got them all in place. We had to be sure all the lights worked.

That was the start of Christmas decorating each year. I displayed all her lovely decorations as instructed. I put a Christmas tree in her patio window and a small one in her hallway. I didn't decorate the tree; I placed all the tree decorations beside each tree. Mum enjoyed putting the decorations on the tree with the aid of her homecare worker. Mum said that it gave them something to do.

I displayed all her decorations where I thought they looked best, just to allow Mum to change them around on a regular basis.

I made a big Christmas dinner with all the trimmings each year. Some years I was able to take Mum to our apartment for dinner. In years when she didn't feel well, I took the dinner to her. Mum wasn't able to go to our apartment for the two years before her death, but we always shared dinner with her.

Her apartment looked beautiful when you walked in during the evening, with minilights sparkling in most of the rooms. I even put minilights in her dining room table centre piece.

Mum enjoyed the Christmas season. When she was able to go out, I would take her for drives to see the beautiful Christmas displays and lights. She would talk about that for days!

We celebrated Thanksgiving as a family, placing a beautiful wreath on Mum's door and preparing a beautiful dinner. I always made extra food when I prepared a celebratory meal. I had learned that from my mother. She wanted to be sure she could feed whoever came by to visit.

Mum's birthdays were special, too. I threw a birthday party for each of her final seven years. We would celebrate her birthday to the fullest with family, friends, food, cake, flowers, and a sprinkling of love over everything.

Early on the morning of Mum's ninety-third birthday, she suffered a ministroke. She was confused for a brief time and needed help to get up. Her coordination wasn't good. I sat with her until her mind cleared and she wanted to get up. She was excited for her birthday celebration, planned for that afternoon.

I had purchased a large cake and ice cream, as well as preparing trays of sandwiches, sweets, fruit, cheese and meat, chips, homemade dips, rolls, and spoon bread. I had also made Mum's favourite punch. There was plenty of food and the celebration was wonderful. We shared the occasion with so many friends and family.

It was the last birthday party I had for Mum.

The next Mother's Day was a quiet family celebration. I was so thankful to still have my mother with me. I gave her a dozen roses and a gift as a token of my love for her. My brothers also came to visit and brought her flowers, plants, and gifts of love.

Visitors always felt at home when they visited Mum. She had a way of making everyone feel welcome.

Mum told me that she couldn't believe my age, because she still considered me to be her little girl. Then she would go on to tell me of how she had loved to dress me in pretty summer dresses and curl my hair in ringlets and take me for walks on the country road to visit my grandfather. To this day, whenever I smell the scent of an orange, I think of my grandfather. I called him Pop. I hold sweet memories of Pop! Mum was surprised that I could remember those days. She said that I was only three or four years old at the time.

My last Mother's Day with Mum.

Twelve

Call 911

While grocery shopping one afternoon in November 2020, my cell phone rang. It was the homecare worker, explaining that she thought Mum had suffered a stroke. I told her to call the ambulance.

I left the grocery cart in the aisle and went straight to Mum's apartment, which was only a short distance away.

When I walked in, I found broken glass and water all over the living room floor. Mum didn't know who I was. She was trying to talk, but her words were garbled. She tried to stand up and point to her chair. She was determined to get into it while the homecare worker cleaned up the spill. It took all my strength to hold Mum back from walking through the glass. I was scared and she had a look of fear on her face.

When the ambulance arrived, Mum couldn't answer many of the paramedics' questions. She was rushed to the hospital and I was right behind them. I was so afraid that I might lose her.

Several tests were done and the diagnosis showed that Mum had suffered not one but two strokes. The doctor put her on a blood thinner. She slept most of that night and the next day. I stayed by her side, in the hope that she would awake and know who I was.

Later the following evening, she opened her eyes. She was confused, giving me a strange look and asking me what had happened.

I was so thankful that she had woken up and could talk. I held her hand and asked if she knew who I was.

She looked at me with that same strange expression. "Well, I should know who you are! You're my daughter, Barbara Ann Parker."

I felt so relieved.

With COVID restrictions in place for hospital visitors, I was only allowed to be with Mum from 2:00 p.m. to 8:00 p.m. Other family members were allowed to visit, but only two at a time.

Mum wanted a phone hooked up. I was reluctant, but she insisted. I knew where this would go—and sure enough, the calls started. She called me in the middle of the night and insisted that I pick her up. She intended to leave the hospital, and if I didn't pick her up she would call a taxi. She wouldn't listen to what I was trying to say. She had gotten it in her head that she wanted out of there. She was so upset with me!

I called the nurses' station and they told me that Mum always seemed fine during the day, but the evenings and nights weren't good. They referred to it as "sundowning." Mum was like a person out of control.

I continued to stay with her during the day, and the calls kept coming at night. On the third night, Mum phoned me and I tried to be stern with her. She was terribly upset and threw the phone on the floor, breaking it. At least that ended the middle-of-the-night calls.

Mum was then placed by the nurses station in a reclining chair, where she slept most nights.

During this period, there was only one incident. An older man wandered the halls day and night. I was told he had Alzheimer's disease and was waiting for placement in a nursing home. Mum was afraid of him.

This night, he passed by a few times and Mum told him to go into his room. The next time he passed, she threw her glass of water at him, according to the nurse. I couldn't imagine my mother doing some of the things she did.

Many changes had to be made before Mum could be released from the hospital. I attended meetings with several professionals and was told I couldn't do this alone. It was recommended that my mother be placed in a nursing home.

When I asked for alternatives, I was thankful that more homecare hours were once again available. They could stay with her from 10:00 a.m. until 8:00 p.m., Monday to Friday, except for one hour between 2:00 p.m. and 3:00 p.m. During that time, I would have to arrange for private care.

It wasn't enough, though. For my mother to go home, I quickly realized that she would require full-time care.

However, Mum wanted to go home. I told the doctor I would stay with her from 8:00 p.m. until 10:00 a.m. when the homecare worker took over. That meant I would also be with her all weekend, every weekend.

After a few weeks, I did arrange for more homecare hours on Saturdays and Sundays. Between my brother helping and hiring private care, we made sure Mum was never alone.

November 2020 marked the beginning of my full-time sleepovers at Mum's place.

I had a promise to keep, and I hoped I could keep it. I prayed a lot, crying myself to sleep many nights. I never wanted Mum to see my fear. I took it one day at a time.

At least Mum was home in her own bed. I slept in the room right next to her. I left a light on in the hallway, a nightlight on in the bathroom, and another one in her bedroom. I tucked her in each night, covering her with her fluffy blanket, kissing her on her cheek, and making sure she had that brass bell within arm's reach in case she needed me during the night. It was a bell my father had brought back when he'd visited the Holy Land. Some nights I didn't even get to my bed before the bell rang. She wanted to know whether the door was locked. Was the coffeepot turned off? How about the fireplace? How about the patio door? This was a nightly routine until I started telling her before I tucked her in that everything was locked and turned off. She would smile. I can picture her lying in bed and reaching up for a goodnight hug. I loved her hugs.

Mum's voice was just a whisper, and it was difficult for some to understand her when she spoke. That was frustrating for Mum. I learned to read her lips.

With COVID affecting so many people during this time, all the activities in our building had to be cancelled. There were no more potluck dinners, no more social gatherings, and very few visitors. Mum made sure I kept her well supplied with hand sanitizer, wet wipes, gloves, disinfectants, and masks. She insisted that everyone who came through her door wear a mask.

Many of the homecare workers were out sick with COVID and Mum was so afraid of getting it. From the time I took her home from the hospital after suffering the strokes, she refused to go outside her apartment—that is, unless it was on a stretcher being pushed by paramedics, taking her to the ambulance for another ride to the emergency room.

The New Bed

That brass bell woke me many nights. I would jump out of bed and run to Mum's room, never knowing what I might find. I lived in constant fear. I can only imagine how Mum felt.

Some nights it was a sick stomach, and I changed her bedding in the middle of the night. Other nights it was a headache, and she needed a painkiller or something to help rid her of gas. The worst nights were those when I entered her room and saw her gasping for air. If the inhalers and mist machine didn't help, I would get on the phone with 911. I made a lot of calls to 911. Mum took a lot of rides in the back of the ambulance. All I could do was pray.

Mum often complained about her bed and didn't want to sleep in it. She couldn't breathe well even though she slept in an upward position with three or more pillows under her head.

I suggested getting a hospital bed for her. I discussed this with family and Mum's family doctor. They agreed it would be beneficial, since Mum could adjust it to her liking and there would be siderails as an added safety feature.

But Mum refused to sleep in a hospital bed. She said that she hated the look of them, they were uncomfortable, and she didn't want one in her bedroom.

"End of discussion," she said.

I had an appointment scheduled with Mum's family doctor, who is also my doctor, the following week. I told him about the hospital bed discussion and he had his secretary set up a phone appointment with my mum. He asked me to be at my mother's apartment when he phoned.

Mum's doctor knew her very well and that phone conversation began casually. Then the doctor asked why she wouldn't allow me to get her a hospital bed. He explained to her that I was trying to help her be more comfortable. Mum listed several reasons as to why she didn't want one, but by the end of the conversation the matter was settled: I ordered the hospital bed to be delivered and set up in Mum's bedroom.

That first night, Mum complained that the bed was too hard and too cold. She didn't like the siderails. I bought a thick foam, a padded mattress cover, pretty flannel sheets, a beautiful bedspread, and an extra warm blanket.

It didn't work. She was determined not to sleep in this bed.

Even with all the padding, fancy sheets, and furry blanket, she only stayed in bed for three hours.

When I heard the bell ring, I ran in and Mum was crying.

I held her and asked what was wrong. She told me that she was afraid to be alone. So I helped her up and wanted to take her into the bedroom next to hers, where I slept when staying in her apartment, so we could sleep together. No. She had a plan. She curled up in the recliner next to my bed. I covered her and tucked the furry blanket under her chin. I even left the lamp on so she could see me.

She slept the rest of the night. She snored and snored.

I gave up trying to get Mum to sleep in that hospital bed. Instead she slept in the recliner next to my bed every night. Worried that she'd get pressure sores from spending so many hours in the recliner, I placed soft pads under her body and behind her back.

When she slept, she relaxed. When she woke up struggling to breathe, it was terrifying.

Fourteen

Don't Sass Me

My heart hurt. Before buying the hospital bed, I wish Mum had told me the real reason she had trouble sleeping. It didn't have anything to do with the bed but with her fear of being alone at night. Why hadn't she told me, I asked her.

"Oh Barb, don't sass me."

Then I cried—and Mum cried because I was crying. But we soon dried our tears and had a cup of tea and Mum sang those famous words: "One day at a time..." Even on the most trying days, Mum and I always ended our days with hugs and kisses.

I will hold the good memories deep in my heart forever: her funny comments, her wishes and demands, our social outings, our craft creations, our knitting sessions, and the times we just sat and browsed through Facebook and Pinterest.

After her hospital stay for the first stroke, I noticed significant changes in Mum's demeanour. She suffered two more ministrokes and it became apparent that her short-term memory was fading. She could remember things from long ago, and she was still quite good at remembering people's names, but she recalled little about things that may have happened the day before. At times she got very confused, which upset her terribly.

Mum's homecare workers were concerned about these changes. They would discuss their concern with me and from time to time ask me to check on her to see what I thought. I always had sweets cooked or new word search books on hand so I had reasons to make discrete visits while her homecare worker was around.

"What are you doing here?" Mum would ask.

I'd chat for a bit, give her a cookie or new book, and then leave if I thought everything was okay. Other times, we decided to call 911.

We had a weekly routine where I gave Mum a shower on Friday evening and washed and set her hair on Saturday morning. The routine became hit-and-miss because Mum was weakening and I was worried about dropping her. I didn't know what I'd do if she fell while I was helping her on and off the shower seat.

So I gave her a sponge bath every day, but she was growing more fragile. It was so sad to see her slowly fade away and lose interest in living. She slept for hours at a time, and some days she would sleep through the homecare worker's entire shift with her. It became clear that I needed more help caring for Mum.

Fifteen

Broken

Mum's mind was broken and my heart was breaking. I started showing signs of my own health issues that needed to be investigated. The doctor ordered tests, scans, bloodwork, and hooked me up to a heart monitor. I do believe that this caused Mum concern and fear.

I hired private care to stay with Mum on nights when I couldn't be with her. This added to my stress and Mum didn't sleep much when I wasn't there.

During the week of my tests, Mum gave me more hugs than she had ever given me before. She was afraid that I wouldn't be able to care for her.

"Oh Barb, don't leave me," she would say.

My doctor was concerned, my brother Richard was concerned, my husband was concerned. I was a mess. I tried to hide my fear from everyone and continue as usual.

One day Richard had a conversation with my doctor, who was also Mum's doctor, and we agreed that he would make a home visit to assess Mum. Mum wasn't too happy to hear that the doctor was coming to see her.

She wasn't feeling very well when the doctor arrived, but she perked up a bit when he told her that I wasn't able to care for her like I had been doing because of my health issues. She became upset and defensive, claiming that she could look after herself.

We all knew that wasn't a possibility.

The doctor then explained that Mum needed to be in a hospital to receive more care than the family could provide. Mum needed access to oxygen.

"And then what?" she asked.

He went on to say that she wouldn't be able to ever return home. She would have to live in an assisting living facility or nursing home. An assessment would be done to determine the level of care needed.

When that assessment was completed, Mum expressed two choices for a nursing home. The doctor submitted this request and further recommended that Mum be admitted to one of two nearby hospitals. Our understanding was that it would only be a short wait.

We gave the landlord a two-month notice on Mum's apartment. In the meantime, we hired more private care, in the form of a woman who would stay overnight with her two nights every week.

We started the process of sorting Mum's things and moving out. She told me what she wanted to take with her to decorate her room when she got to the nursing home. She also chose the clothes she wanted, and the pictures she would hang on her wall, as well as lamps, small tables, and stained-glass ornaments for the window. I neatly stacked these items in the bedroom we no longer used.

As for the rest of her things, she wanted certain items to go to certain people. We were sure to fulfill her wishes.

Then we got a phone call that shocked us. We learned there were no hospital beds available, and the wait for one could be up to six months.

Nonetheless, we pushed on. I promised Mum that I would take her to my place if the hospitals didn't have a bed available when the time came to move from the apartment. The only stipulation was that she would have to sleep in that hard, cold hospital bed with the siderails.

She smiled and hugged me. "No problem, as long as you don't leave me."

I wasn't sure how this would work, but I had a promise to keep, and I was doing my best to keep it. I was willing to stay by Mum's side day and night. I wasn't leaving her.

My husband had recently come home from the hospital after a surgery to remove a kidney stone and he was in great pain from shingles. Yes, I should have been a nurse!

As I recount these memories, I can feel Mum's arms around me. I can hear her faint whisper in my ear. A mother's love is a love like no other.

Sixteen

It Took Her Breath Away

Mum was getting weaker and not eating. In addition to sleeping the day away, she lost interest in doing her word searches. Her eyes hurt when I tried to show her the church service on her tablet. She had always watched church on Sunday mornings, as well as Sunday evenings and Wednesday evenings. She no longer wanted to knit either. She was slowly slipping away.

"It won't be long now," she often said to me.

I knew what she meant. She knew her time was ending. My heart hurt and my eyes leaked every time she said those words. I was so afraid she would die.

I checked again with both local hospitals, but they still didn't have any available beds for people awaiting placement in a nursing home—unless it was an emergency, like a fall causing broken bones or life-threatening illness.

I was shocked. I was so emotional that I couldn't finish these conversations and apologized for calling to inquire. I asked the person on the other end of the line if they believed in prayer; if they did, I asked them to please pray for my mother, whose end-stage COPD was taking her breath away. The disease was life-threatening.

I was so afraid that my mother would die before we were able to get more help. She needed more help than we could give her.

This caused me to reflect to those times when Mum had been physically able to go to the mall and other places with public parking. She'd been my co-pilot, telling me when to go, when to stop, when to slow down, when to turn, and where to park. She had always made me smile, pointing out the parking space in advance. I would hang her handicap sign from the mirror, enter the designated space, and help Mum from the passenger seat.

One time, a grown man approached us after we exited the vehicle. He remarked that neither of us looked like we should be taking up space in a handicapped parking spot.

The comment brought tears to my eyes, but then I got mad.

I found Mum a place to sit inside and then went on a mission to find that man. I didn't owe him an explanation for parking in that spot, but I wanted him to know that my mother suffered from COPD. The handicap sign hanging on the mirror of our car had been prescribed by her doctor. The next time he felt like disrespecting someone in that manner, I wanted him to remember our conversation.

He thanked me for standing up for my mother and then went with me to apologize to Mum.

The first time this happened, I was shocked and appalled. It happened other times, too. We often got nasty comments or funny looks for using handicap parking, but Mum always made me promise that I wouldn't cause a scene. When people made inappropriate comments, I would be able to feel Mum squeezing my arm tight and pushing on me to keep walking.

I just had to refuse to allow other people to steal our joy.

When people made comments like "Your mum looks great!" I always knew they meant well. Mum had a way of hiding her pain and wearing a smile when she was in the company of others.

But the struggle, the pain, the fear was real. COPD is invisible and takes a person's breath away.

Seventeen

Day Six

We were still waiting for a hospital bed for Mum. But on a cold Sunday evening in December 2023, she became very sick, struggling to breathe. Beads of sweat dripped from her forehead and her lips were turning purple.

The ambulance came and took her to the hospital. She was admitted and spent the next five days in the emergency room, due to the lack of beds available.

Thankfully, a bed became available on the third floor on the fifth day.

On the sixth day of her stay, I promised to be back the following morning.

When I walked into the unit on the third floor the next day, I found Mum sitting by the nurses' station. I had a gut feeling that it may have been a rough night for everyone.

I was right. Mum was very confused and told me things that just didn't make sense. She had seen people on the ceiling and letters and words on the wall. She wanted me to clean the walls. She said that it was hurting her eyes.

I spoke to Mum's nurse, who put in a call to the doctor who was caring for my mother. Our family doctor wasn't on call when mum was admitted, but he had assured us that Mum would be well cared for by the doctor who did admit her. He was right. The admitting doctor was lovely and caring.

She assured me that my mother wasn't on any new medications. Mum was only on oxygen to help her breathe.

I sat with Mum each day except Saturday, when my brothers and family visited. Most other days she slept. Then there were those days when she allowed me to give her a sponge bath, then comb her long hair and put it up in a little bun on top of her head. I had to get her changed as quickly as possible afterward because she was weak.

Throughout this hospital stay, I was holding on to hope—but at the same time, I had to face reality.

The nurses had been placing Mum out in the hall by the nurses' desk most nights to ensure her safety. Mum's mind was so confused at night that her personality changed drastically. She wasn't herself at all and behaved unpleasantly when the staff tried to help her.

When I was with her, she was in and out. We could have brief conversations, but then she would start talking about something unrelated to our chat. I would just hold her hand and ask God to please take the confusion from Mum and comfort her.

On day fifteen, Mum woke when I went into her room. We hugged. I lifted my mask and gave her a big kiss on her cheek. Then Mum drifted back to sleep.

I did a few pages in her word search book as she slept.

I noticed Mum moving a little and then the biggest smile came across her face. She opened her eyes and lifted her arms in the air.

I jumped out of my chair. Was Mum was seeing heaven? She kept saying, "Jesus, please... Jesus, please..."

I asked Mum what she was dreaming about and she gave me a funny look.

"Didn't you see Deb?" she asked.

"You must have been dreaming." My sister Deb had passed in 2009.

"I know what I saw."

"And did you see Dad?"

"Yes, I did."

"What was Deb doing?"

"Barb, I wish you could have seen her. She was sitting, reading a book to a group of children, and she didn't have her glasses on."

I knew what Mum was seeing must be real, because my sister had come to me in a dream a year after she'd passed. In that dream, I had asked where her glasses were.

"Barb, you don't need glasses in heaven," she had said to me.

When I asked Mum if she had seen what Dad was doing, she just told me that he'd been sitting there with a funny grin on his face, watching Deb read to the children. Deb had always been Daddy's girl. I can imagine the pride he radiated as he watched his daughter.

Eighteen

Her Wish

On day sixteen, the morning started with pouring rain. While on my way to the hospital, I entered the roundabout a short distance from our home. The car wouldn't steer in the direction I wanted to go, so I had to stop and call my husband.

Larry came to rescue me. He topped up the power-steering fluid in my car and switched vehicles with me. He drove my car back with fluid leaking all the way. My car was the least of my worries at that time. I just wanted to get to my mother.

When I walked in, there she was, sitting in the hallway. I wheeled her down the hall to her room. All the while, she kept looking at me as if she were unsure as to who I was.

"Are you Barb?" she asked.

I pulled down my mask to reassure her that it was me. I told her that I was indeed Barb, her oldest child, and I was there to spend the day with her. She smiled, we hugged, and I tucked her into bed, with some assistance from the attending nurse.

Mum told me of strange things she had been seeing during the night that made her afraid. I believed them to be dreams or hallucinations. She was sure the people from the funeral home had come to her room wanting to cremate her. They'd also wanted to take her eyes out while she was still alive.

She made me promise that I wouldn't allow her to be cremated. I promised her.

She told me many times that she was afraid to die. She also asked me to promise that when she was pronounced dead, I would check and make sure she was dead before I left her. I promised her that I would.

Mum rested for a brief time but seemed restless. She opened her eyes and looked at me frequently, checking to make sure I was still there. She beckoned for me to come close for a hug and I moved close.

"Barb, I wish you were going with me," she said while hugging me. "I am going to miss you."

Mum didn't want to leave her family behind.

I laid on the bed beside her and we hugged. I cried so hard, feeling like a little child in my mother's arms as she kept thanking me for taking care of her. Mum told me to keep being a good girl so she would see me again in heaven.

Mum knew that heaven's doors would soon welcome her home.

Is She Sleeping?

I sat with Mum on day seventeen, as she slept the entire day. There was a larger portable oxygen unit by her bed, with tubes pumping oxygen into my dear mother. The nurses came more often to check her vital signs, but she never woke. She didn't eat or drink that day.

I kissed her cheek and slipped out of her room that evening.

I phoned and spoke to Mum's nurse around 10:00 p.m. and she told me that when she'd gone to check on Mum she had been surprised to see her singing in bed. Mum had then asked for supper and eaten a small portion of applesauce, a couple of bites of toast, and drank a few sips of tea. The nurse told me that Mum was very tired after that and had asked to go back to bed.

I told my husband about this conversation, and we agreed: it was either a good sign or a bad sign. We couldn't tell which.

Early in the morning on the eighteenth day, my phone rang. It was the hospital calling. The doctor told me that Mum wasn't doing well and I should be with her. I was also told what to expect when I got there.

I called the rest of the family and Larry drove me to be with Mum.

Before entering her room, I read the sign written in big letters posted on her door: SANITIZE, WEAR MASKS, GLOVES, SHIELDS, AND GOWNS BEFORE ENTERING THE ROOM. I pulled on the gown, gloves, new mask, and shield. Then I opened the door.

There were machines around her bed. There were nurses and respiratory technicians, all doing what they could to keep Mum comfortable. Mum was struggling to breathe.

My nephew Troy and his sister Melissa, who had just flown from South Carolina, were standing by Mum's bed.

Mum opened her eyes. She may have heard us talking. I told Mum that Melissa was there to see her. Mum looked towards Melissa and shook her head, as though to say, "I can't believe it."

Melissa smiled and kissed Mum gently. Mum closed her eyes and slept.

Richard arrived, and then the doctor assured us that they were doing all they could. She wanted to move Mum to the fourth floor, to a more private room where the family could be with her. We agreed.

It was a lovely room and Mum continued to sleep. There was nothing we could do. I felt so helpless.

I phoned the family members who couldn't be there, holding the phone to Mum's ear so they could tell Mum they loved her and say their final goodbyes.

We cried, we prayed, and we sang to her and told her we loved her. We talked, we held her hand, we kissed her sweet cheeks, and we whispered in her ear. We didn't want her to go.

Early that evening, on December 27, 2023, Mum took her last breath.

Twenty

Take the Picture

I miss my mother every day. So many things remind me of her. Writing this book has been a labour of love. My puffy eye have leaked throughout the countless hours of typing and retyping, but the tug at my heartstrings has compelled me to keep going. I've chose to share about the seven years I cared for Mum to encourage other families to cherish every moment they can spend with their mothers, who gave them life.

Tell your Mum that you love her. Show her love and compassion.

Take tons of pictures. You will be thankful you did.

I have pictures I can look at and allow myself to live in that special moment.

There are three comments Mum used to make that will be forever embedded in my mind. She often reminded me of these words:

"Barb, please don't leave me."

"Remember, I'm the boss."

"One day at a time."

Yes, I cherish those memories. I'm a strong woman today because a strong woman raised me!

Twenty-One

Family and Friends

Mum's funeral was held on January 2, 2024. We waited until my brother Billy and his son Eric could fly in from North Carolina.

The celebration of Mum's life was beautiful. The music was touching. The speakers who shared had known Mum for years. They spoke of their many special times with Mum. Richard gave the eulogy. His words touched many, fulfilling Mum's wish for him to speak at her funeral. Mum would have been so proud of him.

A small catered reception was held in a spacious room at the funeral home, where we met relatives and friends whom we hadn't seen since Dad's funeral.

Before the reception was over, and before people left, I made my way around the room with my faithful basket. I handed out Mum's scrubbies,[1] the ones she had made with her own hands. Mum loved giving her scrubbies to people who came to visit her.

---
[1] These were pot scrubbers and dishcloths.

Mum and Dad's wedding photo.

Twenty-Two

Feathers from Heaven

One Mother's Day, I wanted to get my mother something she would love and cherish. Something pink caught my eye: a music jewellery box. I knew this was the gift I was looking for and the song it played was "Wind Beneath My Wings."

Mum loved her gift. "Oh, Barb, I love it. And look! It matches the colours in my living room."

She placed it on the end table next to her sofa. Often she opened the cover and listened to the music as it played that beautiful song.

We chose to display some of Mum's favourite things on a table at the funeral home. We placed her Bible, her word search book, and the pen she used to complete her last page of searching for words. We also included her glasses, pictures of her and Dad, and a beautiful angel that had been given to her by one of her grandsons, James.

And yes, we placed her music box there.

After the funeral, the items were given to family members, and I chose the pink music box for myself. I took the music box home and placed it on my dresser next to the picture of Deb and a picture of Mum and Dad.

The following week, as I was cleaning out Mum's apartment, I decided to get on my stepladder and doublecheck the high shelves of the closets and cupboards.

On the top shelf of Mum's bedroom closet, I found something tiny and shiny. Upon examining it more closely, I saw that it was a silver broach in the shape of a feather. I don't know how I had missed it when I cleaned before.

I shared the story with Richard, Jerry, and Christine, who were at the apartment with me. I told them that it was a sign from Mum and she would be coming back to visit me in the form of a feather. We wiped the tears, hugged, and then I took the broach home and placed it in the pink music box.

At that moment, I realized that the music box had feathers painted on the top, along the sides, and on the back. It also occurred to me that the song, "Wind Beneath My Wings," was a close reference to feathers.

Here I was placing Mum's broach in the shape of a feather in Mum's music box covered in painted pink feathers.

A few days later, while coming out of the mall, I looked down and saw a fluffy white feather on the ground. I froze and got goosebumps as tears trickled down my cheeks.

"Is that you, Mum?" I whispered.

I started walking away, since there were people coming and going all around me, but I felt compelled to stop and go back. Finding that the feather was still there, I leaned over and picked it up. People may have wondered why I would pick up this feather. If they only knew!

I took this fluffy white feather and put it in the music box as well.

A few days later, while walking out of a bank on the other side of town, I looked down and saw another fluffy white feather on the ground.

Did I pick it up?

I sure did!

I didn't care who saw me. I knew that this was Mum, letting me know that she was watching over me.

I took that feather home and put it, too, in the pink music box.

I'm now anxiously awaiting my next encounter with Mum as she sends another feather to assure me that she's watching over me. Feathers appear when angels are near.

> I'm an angel feather
> Sent from God above
> To serve as a reminder
> Of His precious love.
> I'm from your
> Guardian angels that
> God assigned to you
> And fell out in their
> Struggles as they
> Protected you.
> Each time you almost fall,
> Thank God and all His angels
> For answering your call.

Mum's feather broach.

Mum knitting.

Conclusion

I chose to author this book in honour of my mother, Geneva Mae Arbeau, who went to her heavenly home on December 27, 2023. She will surely have enjoyed her heavenly reunion with so many friends and loved ones who went before her. In this book, I've shared the last seven years of Mum's life with those who are still with us and miss Mum as much as I do.

For those who relate to her as a mum, gram, nan, aunt, sister, best friend, pastor's wife, or friend, I want to say thank you for loving her. My mother loved people! She loved to celebrate people she looked forward to any reason to hold a social event.

If you knew my mother, I can be certain that you attended one of her social events or enjoyed afternoon tea at her home. Or maybe you enjoyed one of her beautiful home-cooked meals. Or maybe you were gifted a scrubbie or two when you visited her.

My father, Rev. Willis Arbeau, was born and raised in Grey Rapids on the Miramichi River. My mother was raised by her grandparents in Durham Bridge, New Brunswick. When my parents married, they resided in Grey Rapids.

Our family moved to Marysville, a suburb of Fredericton, when I was nine years old. It was a big transition for our family. I went from a one-room schoolhouse to a big school with separate rooms and specialized teacher for each class. My father worked at the Chestnut Canoe Factory and my mother cleaned offices in the evenings. My father was incredibly involved in church work and my mother supported him every step of the way.

When I turned sixteen in 1964, my father became pastor of his first church. We packed up and moved to a small railway town, McAdam.

We settled in quite nicely there and my parents made many new friends. The people were friendly and I lived there for three years.

However, I found it a bit awkward fitting into the new school. I started high school being tagged as the preacher's daughter.

Three days after graduating high school, I moved back to the Fredericton area where I had accepted a government job.

My youngest brother Billy started Grade One in McAdam. On the first day, he decided that he didn't like school and walked home during morning recess. He told Mum that he quit. Mum had other plans for that young boy and marched him right back to the school. He never tried that again.

Our family made many great friends in McAdam and those friendships remain in place for those of us who are still living. We hold wonderful memories of the many who have passed.

After seven or eight years, my parents moved to the town of Caribou in Maine, where my father pastored a church. The congregation grew over a brief period and a new church was built during that time.

My two youngest brothers were still living at home when my parents moved to Caribou. They made lots of friends and left an impression wherever they went. Both boys eventually made their way back to Fredericton.

My sister married an American and continued living in Maine. I visited my family in Caribou often and was fortunate to meet many friends of my family.

The next move for my parents was to Edmundston, back in New Brunswick. Imagine moving to a French-speaking city and not being able to speak or understand the language! Some of their new friends were bilingual, fortunately, and my father had a translator for his church services. My parents did well and enjoyed their time there.

Next, they came back to the Fredericton area, with my parents purchasing a home in Marysville. I helped with the move and unpacking and setting up their new home. They were ready for retirement and a slower pace of life.

No matter where my parents and family lived, we were fortunate to meet so many wonderful people. The people we called friends often contacted me over the years to inquire about Mum in the seven years after Dad passed. One dear friend, Doris, who met my mother in Caribou but now lives in Oklahoma, stayed connected with Mum during her illness. They enjoyed many video chats.

I trust that all these friends, family, and family of friends have enjoyed reading this account of the last seven years of my mother's life as seen through my eyes, her loving daughter Barb.

Appendix:
Memories of a Special Lady

For this book, I invited many family members and friends of my mother to contribute their special memories of Mum. I wish to thank all of those who chose to share their memories and kind words.

Although my mother is no longer with us, her light will continue to shine through these memories of love and laughter. My heart has been touched, my tears have flowed, and I feel blessed as I prepared these words for publication. I trust you will feel that love as you turn the following pages.

I will begin by sharing a couple memories.

I was in my teens and all my friends were wearing tartan skirts. So I asked my mother if she thought I could have one for Christmas.

At that time, my father was pastoring his first church and his income was low. But we always had food to eat, clothes to wear, and a roof over our head. I never expected to get a tartan skirt for Christmas, but it was nice to dream.

On Christmas morning, a Sunday, my brothers, my sister, and I opened our gifts as Mum and Dad stood close by. Mum handed me my last gift. When I opened it, I found myself looking down at the tartan skirt I had been dreaming about.

I was so excited to try it on! It fit perfectly. I decided to wear it to church that morning for sure and asked Mum if she would wear her own tartan skirt to church also.

"Not today," she said.

I begged her to please wear her skirt that morning so we would match. That's when Mum took me aside and told me that she didn't have a tartan skirt anymore. She explained that she had taken her tartan skirt apart and used the fabric to make a tartan skirt for me.

I felt so bad that I cried. We hugged and I thanked her for being so kind and thoughtful. Mum was so proud to provide me with that tartan skirt!

To some, this may not mean much, but to me it's a story of a mother's love.

The next beautiful memory is one that Richard shared with me about a time when he sat with Mum. When he was visiting Mum in the hospital in December 2023, she was so upset and scared as she struggled to breathe.

"I don't know what to do," she said.

"What do you mean?" he asked.

"I know that I won't be going back to my apartment, but I want to live. I love my family and don't want to leave them. I'm going to die here in the hospital."

Richard turned to Mum. "We love you, too, and we don't want to see you suffer. You have a great hope. Jesus will take you in His arms. Deborah and Dad will be waiting for you."

"I know that," she replied, "but I told God that I want to live until my children and my grandchildren are saved."

Richard told me that this was heartbreaking. When he told Mum that he had to leave, she begged him to stay longer.

"I am so lonely," she said.

So he stayed.

About forty minutes passed, and then he told her that he needed to leave to drive back to Saint John. But she asked him to stay a little longer.

He stayed with her for another twenty minutes or so. After that, he assured her that Jerry and Christine were coming to be with her. He decided to pray with her before he left to go home.

Richard held Mum's hand and asked God to fill her heart with His beautiful peace, allowing her to feel His arms around her and His presence in her hospital room.

They cried and prayed together. Then he gave Mum a gentle hug, and she hugged him back. They said goodbye and Richard left her room. He tried not to show his tears as he exited the elevator in the hospital lobby.

Richard arrived home at about 4:30 p.m. that day. After talking to his wife Shirley for a few minutes, he decided to take his dog Lady for a walk. He was still feeling sad for Mum in the hospital and prayed for God to take her home so she wouldn't have to continue to suffer.

God spoke to him: *"Remember the message that Pastor Woodward preached at your father's funeral? Prayers never die."*

"But I do," Richard responded.

God told him that he could tell his mother that her prayers would be answered, that her children and grandchildren would be saved. She could go home.

When Mum was moved to the palliative care unit on December 27, 2023, God reminded Richard of the conversation he'd had with Mum a few days before.

As we all sat with Mum, knowing that her time on earth was coming to an end, we sang, prayed, and held her hand. We hugged her, kissed her, and told her how much we loved her.

As Richard was hugging Mum, he whispered in her ear to repeat what the Lord had spoken to him. He assured her that her prayers would be answered. She could now rest in peace and go to be with Jesus, Dad, and Deborah.

"They're watching and waiting for you," he whispered. "There will be no more pain and sorrow. I will miss you dearly, but I want you to go and be with Jesus. I don't want you to suffer anymore. I promise to meet you soon."

Richard left the room shortly after that, knowing that it would be the last time he saw our mother alive.

Only twenty minutes later, I phoned Richard to tell him that Mum had completed her earthly journey.

Richard and Mum.

Richard Arbeau (Son)

When my sister asked if I would like to write some special memories of our mother to be included in her book, my mind was flooded with memories. I recall many of my childhood years and of how my mother was always there for me through my teens and into adulthood.

I recall my mother getting me ready for Sunday school. She took pride in ensuring that I was always dressed nice, my hair combed perfectly. She would also check to make sure my ears were clean and my teeth brushed. We were to be seen and not heard. If we acted up, we knew what to expect when we got home.

When we were living in Marysville and I was in preschool, my father accepted a job as pastor of the Pentecostal Church in McAdam. My mother always sent me with my dad on his weekend trips to McAdam. She said it was to keep him company.

We would leave on Friday after Dad got off work at the Chestnut Canoe Factory and return home on Monday morning. I remember missing Mum and feeling alone while my father prepared his Sunday sermons.

On the drive back on Mondays, without failure, Dad would always say, "Giddy-up, car. Get us home fast so Richard can see Mum." He knew I missed Mummy.

I have another childhood memory from when we lived in McAdam. We would travel to Fredericton so Mum could go to Zellers and pay for Christmas gifts that she had on a layaway plan with her monthly child benefit cheque. Mum was a planner. She always made sure we enjoyed a nice Christmas.

There always seems to be visitors at our home. Mum was a great cook and prepared lovely meals for all. She would keep busy serving everyone, but she never prepared a plate for herself until the others were ready for dessert. I often wondered why Mum kept herself busy at the cupboard while everyone was enjoying her great meal—that is, until late in life. When I asked her this question, she told me that she had wanted to make sure there was enough food to feed everyone else first.

Seeing large boxes of Ganong assorted chocolates takes me back to my childhood days. When Christmastime was near, a friend would give Mum a large red box of chocolates, which she would hide in the top of her bedroom closet.

Oh boy, was I excited to see that red box! Each day I would get up on a chair, open that sweet box, and take one chocolate. Just one. Each day I looked forward to feeding my sweet tooth. I would have to tell myself not to take more than one, but soon it was too late and half the box was gone.

When Mum opened the box at Christmastime, she was shocked. But no one admitted to the theft.

Later in life, when I was at an extremely low place in my life, I called my mother in desperation. I wanted to change doctors, since I needed more help than I was getting. Mum called a woman she knew who worked for a doctor and explained my situation. That doctor agreed to take me as a patient, and I got the help I needed to get back on my feet.

My mother loved her children and would do whatever she could do to help them. I am so thankful for a loving mother.

As Mum aged and struggled with her health, I'm thankful that I was able to be there to help my sister care for her.

Until we meet again. Rest in peace, Mum.

Billy Arbeau (Son)

When Barb asked if I would like to share a special memory of our mother, I instantly thought about my unexpected Christmas gift. We were living in Caribou, Maine, where my father was pastor of a church. I knew my parents didn't have a lot of money, but they were always able to provide the necessities.

I was young, in fourth grade, and one day my mother and I were in a large department store. I spotted a pair of cowboy boots I really liked. Mum allowed me to try them on, but she told me that she couldn't afford to buy them.

I sulked a bit, because I liked those boots.

On Christmas morning, I got the best surprise when I opened that box. There were the cowboy boots I had tried on in the store that day with Mum.

I didn't ask any questions about how she was able to buy the boots for me. I wore them with pride.

Our mother did what she could to help provide for her children. She sold crafts, made and sold baked goods, made and sold peanut brittle, and kept children in our home. Mum was thrifty and knew how to stretch a dollar.

Karla Kennedy (Granddaughter)

I cherish many memories of Gram. From when I was a little girl, Gram would come to visit. We were always anxious to see what she brought for us. One thing that stands out in my memory is the bottles of pink strawberry fluff she brought from Maine, because we couldn't buy it in Canada. We sure loved when Gram came to visit!

One time when Gram and Gramp came to visit for the weekend, Gram was headed to the living room to sit in her favourite swivel rocking chair. She was on a mission to get to that chair before anyone else.

She plunked herself down in that chair so hard and so fast that the chair tipped over backwards into the corner. All we could see was her little feet with red fuzzy footies kicking in the air.

She called out for us to help her, but we were all laughing so hard that it took us a bit to get her and the chair in an upward position.

Gram and I always had a good laugh when we talked about that incident in her later years.

One time our family took Gram with us to Disney World in Florida. We walked around, enjoyed all the sites, and saw birds flying everywhere above us. Suddenly, Gram stopped and felt the bun on top of her head.

"That bird pooped in my bun," she said.

It was funny to me, but it wasn't funny to Gram. Mum took Gram into the washroom and washed the mess out of her hair and fixed her bun just the way Gram wanted it.

Gram sometimes came to stay with us children when my parents went away. One time was because my mother was in the hospital having my youngest sister. Another time Mum was in the hospital having surgery.

Gram made us mind her, but she loved us dearly.

Whenever I see a dish of Jello, I think of her. When Gram watched over us, there were always small dishes of Jello in the fridge. We would open the fridge for a snack when we came home from school and Gram would say, "Just have a dish of Jello. Your supper will be ready soon."

Just a few months before Gram passed, I visited her at her apartment. Sure enough, she had small dishes of Jello in her fridge. She enjoyed toast and Jello for a snack.

Gram loved her Jello.

Gloria M. Clark (Friend)

> When my thoughts drift to this lady
> I try with a few words to describe
> What I learned as I observed
> Her final miles on earth.

G—She was a Giver. Time, talent, and treasure poured into others.

E—What she did, she did with Excellence. Be it entertaining or decorating, all was mastered to her perfection.

N—No-nonsense Geneva took her Christian faith and the Bible seriously. She was unwavering.

E—She was Elegant. She presented herself with class.

V—She was Vivacious, full of fun, and added spark to any gathering. She loved to laugh.

A—She was an Adoring mother and grandmother. I remember how I could see the love and pride in her eyes when she showed off pictures of her loved ones. She was rooting for all of you.

Tammy Arbeau (Daughter-in-Law)

Many of the memories I have of my mother-in-law are ones of laughter and sharing.

One that stands out is the time when she and Gramp came to visit our family in North Carolina. I think it may have been in 1994. I recall the love she shared as she spent time with our children and the fun we had as she showed me how to cook things her way. I just loved how she wore her apron and made everything look so easy. She was a great cook.

I admired her so much. She was like a second mother to me.

Rest in peace, sweet lady.

Shirley Arbeau (Daughter-in-Law)

One memory that holds a place in my heart for my mother-in-law, Geneva, is that whenever she and papa came to visit, she always brought treats for everyone.

When our children Candace and Joel were small, only nineteen months apart, Geneva was always willing to help. She was an immense help during Harvey Camp meeting time[2] in the summers, when the children were young.

I have special memories of when we lived in Edmundston and having the children's grandparents living nearby. Geneva loved her grandchildren and showed her love in many ways throughout the years.

Geneva enjoyed having her whole family join her for birthday parties and special occasions. It was a time of sharing love and laughter. We will miss those unique events.

Rest in peace. Until we meet again.

---

[2] At Harvey Camp meeting times, people from all over gathered for fellowship of worship.

Eric Arbeau (Grandson)

Growing up, we didn't get to see Grandma often. We live in North Carolina and Grandma lived in New Brunswick, Canada.

Memories I hold dear to my heart are of the times when we were young and she came to visit. Grandma would want all of us kids to sit—or pile on her, I should say. She enjoyed showering us with love.

I never remember her having a bad moment. She was cheerful, full of laughter, and so loving when we were around her.

There aren't too many people who stand out to me as I was growing up. I guess you would call it an unfiltered deep love of everyone she knew and cared for. It poured out of her every day she was with us. It was the kind of love that flowed when she was in the room. Grandma was a sweet, loving lady.

Don Estey (Nephew)

Aunt Geneva's life, words, and daily actions were a testament to a life well lived. She lived solely for a testimony to her Lord Jesus.

Auntie, you may be gone from this earth, but your spirit will live on forever, until I too will behold Him. Rest in peace.

Larry Parker (Son-in-Law)

When my wife asked if I'd like to share special memories of my mother-in-law, Geneva, my thoughts immediately went back to the many times she struggled with health issues over the past seven years.

It was sad to watch the changes in her demeanour. I found it hard when I went to see her and she couldn't talk. I always wondered what she was thinking. I would sit with her and hold her hand.

One thing I will cherish forever is how she rubbed the top of my hand while we held hands, looking at me with her beautiful smile.

When I first met her years ago, she was a vibrant, outgoing, busy lady who loved to travel. She visited with us on Grand Manan a few times. She didn't like the ferry ride, but that didn't stop her. She was intrigued with watching the whales from our front deck facing the ocean.

I recall the beautiful baskets she made for us at Christmastime. They were full of her homemade jams, pickles, cookies, cakes, peanut brittle, fudge, and my favourite licorice candy.

Mum was an excellent cook. Any time we went to visit her and Dad, she insisted that we have something to eat. Her fridge was always full of goodies.

When my wife was caring for her, she would say to Barb, "Take some of that home to Larry. He would like that." She loved to share.

There were times when I was sick while Barb cared for her mother. Mum was concerned and always wanted to know how I was feeling.

We try to focus on the good memories of family gatherings, the laughs we had, her funny comments, and the joy and love she shared with each one of us. Mum was a special lady. I am thankful for the opportunity to be part of her family.

Until we meet again, stay sweet.

Bonnie Cross (Friend)

My sweet friend Geneva was such a caring mother and a wonderful helpmate to her husband.

She appeared at times to be quiet and reserved, but we saw right through her, she was a softy and very witty. We shared many laughs together as we reminisced about years gone by and all the fun times we had with family and friends.

I enjoyed spending evenings with Geneva and Barb, sipping on our tea and discussing times gone by. It was a joy to be a part of Geneva's birthday celebrations.

It was always a pleasure to visit with Geneva. She had a way of making me feel right at home. She had known my mother, Grace, for many years and often spoke of all the great times and laughter she shared with my mother.

Geneva will certainly be missed, and her memories will live on forever.

Doris Hapke (Friend)

I hold so many good memories in my heart of my dear friend Geneva. She was a loyal friend.

We met when the Arbeau family moved to Caribou, Maine. I have great memories of the fun times our family shared with Sister Arbeau and her family.

She and I always went out together on Fridays. That was our day to have fun, whether we were having lunch, hair appointments, and of course doing a little shopping. We always cooked together for the holidays, which was so much fun. I loved her so much.

In recent years, after Barb started caring for her mother, she would set Sister Arbeau and me up in front of the video screen. It was a real joy to see her face as we chatted. We will have a great reunion in heaven one day.

> Your mother's light
> Still shines
> Her light still shines
> In memories
> Of love and laughter shared
> In all the ways
> She touched your life
> And all the ways she cared

Charlie Meade (Friend)

I am blessed to have known Geneva. Whenever she and I would meet at church or on the street, she always greeted me with the biggest smile. She was a powerful lady with the spirit of encouragement in abundance.

She always greeted me in a most gracious manner. She would touch my cheek and say it was good to see me again. Her presence always gripped my heart and made me feel so special.

We had a spiritual kinship like no other. She had influence in my life with her gentleness and genuine caring spirit. Her occasional hug was like Jesus hugging me. She made my heart smile every time we met.

She carried a special anointing that changed the course of many lives for the good, including mine. I will always remember her with great fondness. Rest in peace.

Vera O'Donnell (Best Friend)

Geneva and I were best friends for seventy years. We had so many great times together and I have wonderful memories that I will treasure forever. She was a loyal friend I could always count on. I miss her and treasure the memories.

Until we meet again.

Valerie Sawler (Friend)

When I think of Geneva, I have so many wonderful memories. My mother and Geneva were great friends from the time when I was a small child. I'll never forget all the times I spent at Geneva's home. She always made me feel at home, treating me like one of her own.

I deeply miss her and our visits, which always included a cup of tea. She was a great lady.

Weldon Laking (Friend)

It was more than just another birthday. When I turned fourteen, our home church in McAdam, New Brunswick was getting a new pastor, a family of five plus their parents. They didn't know it yet, but the family was about to get bigger.

It wasn't long before I was welcome at the kitchen table, at the pastor's house. I was welcome in their living room and even welcome as a guest in the little front porch. I was special. Brother Arbeau called me son and Sister Arbeau called me son, Weldon, and other names. When she called me Weldon, it wasn't always to the table for supper.

I am so thankful that I'm still considered part of the family.

I'm so grateful for my Christian heritage. I was raised in church, and I mean every service. If the church doors were open, our family was there. We lived about a mile from the church, on the "other side of the tracks," yet Mother checked to be sure we were clean behind the ears and properly dressed in our church clothes.

I had the very best natural birth mother and I miss her so. Being the child I was, the Lord knew I needed two mothers, so he gave me a bonus mum: Sister Arbeau. I have always called her Mum, and to my adopted siblings I say a big thank you for sharing your mum with me.

When Brother Arbeau became pastor in McAdam in 1964, I was just fourteen. His son Jerry and I became very close friends. Therefore, I was in their home often. There were a few times I was told, "Weldon, when you leave, turn the lights out and lock the outside door."

Jerry and I were typical teenagers most of the time. Then there were times when we were daring and mischievous, which usually led to us having to deal with Mum Arbeau.

Sister Arbeau had a gift of knowledge. I'm not sure how, but she always knew what we were doing if we were involved in any type of misbehaviour. She had her way to bring it to my attention and would want an explanation. She didn't tolerate misbehaviour. I even got a swat with the flyswatter a few times.

However, she knew how to measure out love during times of correction. "Come sit over here," she would say. I always knew what was about to happen. It was time for the hearing. Court was in session.

Some of her questions, I wouldn't answer. I couldn't, I wouldn't, I shouldn't tell everything. Times like these, I discovered, were difficult. I felt that teenagers had a different view and different preferences. Sometimes I was allowed to explain mine, but most often it was best to listen. Many times, we weren't on the same page. But after these discussions, she would pat me on the back of my hand and say, "Now you behave. Make your mother proud of you."

As I grew old enough to seriously consider going to Bible college, my life and my surroundings began to change. When I received my letter of acceptance, Sister Arbeau became my encourager. She urged me to apply myself and behave myself.

The church celebrated me with a party. Brother Arbeau gifted me with a concordance and a dictionary. Sister Arbeau gave me a personal gift. I was hardly old enough to grow a fair crop of fuzz for facial hair, but she gave me my very first bottle of aftershave, which I kept for years.

In the early spring of my second semester, word filtered to Sister Arbeau that I had a crush on a young lady at the Bible College in Fredericton. Even back in 1969, there were whistleblowers.

Sister Arbeau gave her stamp of approval of this young lady I had fallen for, and it is now fifty-five years later and she and I are so thankful for Sister Arbeau's prayers and overflowing heart of love. She helped us through some rough times.

Brother and Sister Arbeau were there to console me when my brother was killed in an industrial accident in Ontario. They were the ones to bring me the sad news when I was still in Bible college. Sister Arbeau held me close and let me cry. Tears are a language only God understands. Her warm tears mingled with mine as she patted my hand. Brother Arbeau wrapped me in his strong arms and prayed. His voice gave me peace. They took me home and were there for me through the difficult days.

We all learned that Sister Arbeau was a very special lady. I believe her speciality was compassion and love for all of us. I just happened to be blessed with abundance. There were many times when I needed correction, but she knew that the pat on my hand was more effective than a slap on the wrist.

As we roll back the curtain of memory, she will never be forgotten. Her beaming face, love, and contagious smile will always be remembered. We loved her.

I marvel at how God orchestrated my steps and gave me Sister Arbeau, a priceless ruby to guide my footsteps, as well as my thinking. He gave me the very best second mum.

My sincere thanks to Barb, Jerry, Debbie, Richard, and Billy for the years of treating me like family and sharing your precious mum with me. She is still working on me. Sometimes I think I hear a soft voice say, "Behave. Make sure your mother will be proud of you." I will never forget her light pat on the back of my hand.

Rev. Jack Leaman (Friend)

It is with much fondness, mixed with a strong sense of mourning, that we take a moment to remember this wonderful lady that represents much of our Christian heritage.

Through my entire life, I have been a part of the Atlantic District United Pentecostal Church and I have had the privilege of continually crossing paths with Geneva.

In my reflections of her life, I can confirm that she always had a concern for others, a celebration with others, and a personal determination to do the work and will of the God she served, regardless of the personal cost.

Her frequent communication about what was happening in her family conveyed her strong love for each of them. Her lifelong support emotionally and spiritually for her husband was so precious to see.

Her prayers for all of us were invaluable.

Her consistent encouragement to everyone was irreplaceable.

As her health weakened, her faith strengthened.

Her lifelong testimony is a true tribute to the goodness of God. Her deep impact here will continue to be felt into eternity.

I thank God for this precious lady of faith.

The Arbeau family.

Mum and Dad on their anniversary.

Mum's Molasses Cookies

This is my mother's recipe for molasses cookies. Several people have commented on these cookies over the years and I've shared it with many. Enjoy!

1 cup of soft shortening (I use margarine)
1 cup of white sugar
1 cup of molasses
1 egg (beaten)
¾ cup of hot water (dissolve 4 tsp. baking soda)
1 tsp. of cloves
1 tsp. of cream of tartar
1 tsp. of salt
1 tsp. of ginger
5 cups of flour

Mix shortening, molasses, sugar, ginger, salt, egg, and cloves together. Sprinkle cream of tartar overtop. Add hot water/baking soda. Mix well. Add flour.

Chill for a half-hour. Roll out and use cookie-cutter.

I add a little sugar on top of the cookies before baking.

Place on floured cookie sheet. Bake at 350 degrees for approximately ten to twelve minutes. Ovens vary in temperature. I test by touch; if the cookie bounces back, it is cooked.

Cookies should be fluffy and tasty. Do not overcook.

Other titles by Barbara Parker:

My Sister's Journey from Headache to Heartache (2010)
The Choice: My Path, My Destiny (2013)

www.ingramcontent.com/pod-product-compliance
Lightning Source LLC
LaVergne TN
LVHW051500070426
835507LV00022B/2850